Matt Gupta

THE FOUR
ANGELS

THE FOUR ANGELS

By Matt Gryta

Getzville Grove Press, Ltd.
TOLEDO, OHIO

All photos courtesy Buffalo Courier-Express Archive, E. H. Butler Library, SUNY College at Buffalo

First Publication 2018

Getzville Grove Press, Ltd.
Toledo, Ohio 43604
www.getzvillegrove.com

Book Layout ©2017 BookDesignTemplates.com

Ordering Information:
Quantity sales. Special discounts are available on quantity purchases by corporations, associations, and others. For details, contact the "Special Sales Department" at the address above.

The Four Angels/Matt Gryta. -- 1st ed.
ISBN 978-0-9911057-4-8

Prologue

L ike the crucifixion of Jesus of Nazareth thousands of years earlier, the maternal crucifixions of Kylia, Amina, Inez and Demario Trait belatedly changed the lives of many. Though the physical and emotional abuse of children in the Buffalo, New York area of the United States of America continued for decades and decades after their deaths, the impulses to prevent such horrors because of their murders helped shaped local government policy, just as the death of Jesus, considered The Christ by many, shaped spiritual views for millennia.

CHAPTER ONE

Absolute Horror

D ear Lord of thee -- three things I pray: To know they more clearly; To love thee more dearly and to serve thee more nearly," Kylia Person Trait, 9, a third-grader at Buffalo, New York's Public School 8 wrote in May 1978.

"Love is the sweetest thing of all," she also wrote on what was to be a greeting card to her father, Joseph Person. She had hoped to at least belatedly give it to him as a Father's Day gift that summer.

She never did.

That card and the child's prayer to The Lord were among her school papers found by the court-appointed foster mother she and her three half-siblings had lived with until May 7, 1978. Their mother, Gail Trait, regained custody ten days before she ritually hacked them to death in a voodoo-like ceremony with a 13-inch butcher knife and a 7-inch paring knife.

Kylia Trait   Amina Trait

Inez Trait   Demario Trait

Kylia and her half-siblings had moved from 39 Victoria Avenue with their mother to the second floor flat of Trait's mother's mother, Dorothy Williams, at 122 Montana Avenue on July 15, 1978.

Now-retired Buffalo Police Lt. Larry Baehre in December 2016 recalled how he and now-retired Lt. John M. Rooney were among the first uniformed officers to arrive at the Montana Avenue site after an urgent 911 call had been made the night of the killings.

Driving from a call in the city's Jefferson Avenue area Baehre and Rooney arrived on Montana to see officers from the police department's Tactical Patrol Unit and Buffalo firefighters already dealing with an African-American woman who was literally covered in blood.

The firefighters, there to treat any wounded victims, told news media representatives they had been puzzled because the bloody woman, who turned out to be Gail Trait, did not seem to have any wounds on her body.

When Police Officers Jim Jackson and Steve Evans arrived in their patrol car they, Baehre and Rooney began walking up the stairs to the second floor flat. Those four officers had been told that's where the incident took place.

"We climbed the stairs single file, we all unholstered our service revolvers," Baehre told the author in December 2016.

"As we got to the second floor landing the door to the flat was open. Very cautiously we entered. We called out something like POLICE, ANYONE HERE?" Getting no response we went inside," he said.

"In the living room we saw two little children on the floor covered in blood and obviously dead. The TV was on in the room and cast an eerie light into the room. When we got to the kitchen it was a very startling and horrific sight," Baehre said.

"There was blood all over the floor, there were pots and pans filled with blood, knives, an anatomy book on the kitchen table, as well as the dismembered body parts of small children and two more little kids dead on the kitchen floor."

"At this time, we were thinking that the perpetrator of all this was still in the flat," he added.

"We were all thinking that any moment someone was going to jump out of one of the other rooms in the apartment and try to attack us."

"As we were making our way across the kitchen we were actually slipping and sliding in the coagulated blood on the floor. As you can imagine, we were very cautious in our search of the other rooms in the apartment," Baehre continue.

Finding no one else in the second floor flat Baehre said the officers began assessing the entire scene, which he described as "the most gruesome crime scene that I had ever seen ...and the worst one I saw in the rest of my 32 years" in the police department.

Baehre said he and every other officer at the Montana Avenue crime scene had only feelings of "absolute horror and revulsion at what we saw."

Outside the house while everyone waited for the ambulance that would take Gail Trait to a hospital for whatever treatment she needed, Lt. Rooney, then a platoon leader in Precinct 12, interviewed Trait, Baehre said.

"It was at that time that she mentioned something about Voodoo to him," which became an element of the prosecution case early in the investigation, he noted.

Baehre's shift ended at 8 a.m. that day. When he went home that day he did not tell his wife and daughter that he had been one of the first officers at what he called that "unbelievable crime."

Days later he told them about the incident, but never described to them what he had seen in the upstairs flat.

"I can still remember," Baehre said in December 2016 "that night and the unbelievable sight of those innocent lilt dead children who were killed and cut up by their own mother in such a savage manner."

"As a police officer, it's something that you have to block out when you're on the job, but as a human being it's something that stays with you forever," he said.

Baehre said the only thought that gives him any comfort in recalling the Trait incident was that the four children "are resting in a much better place."

James Jackson wrote to Baehre in December 2016 about being at the Trait flat hours after the murders.

In his letter to Baehre he called that incident "without a doubt the most traumatic event of my entire career.....I recall our first minutes in the upper flat with those poor kids' bodies, attempting to visually and mentally process those savage wounds. We had to look for the possible killer, thinking "he" was still in the apartment, finally clearing the apartment and realizing that the monster that had butchered these innocents was sprawled out on the lower porch when we had initially arrived," Jackson wrote.

Baehre became the police department's first public information officer and held that post for the last five years of his 32-year career. That public information job was created by then Buffalo Police Commissioner Gil Kerlikowske.

Kerlikowske later became Seattle police commissioner and then, under President Obama, served as commissioner of the U.S. Customs and Border Protection agency, the largest law enforcement agency of the U.S. Department of Homeland Security.

Mrs. Dorothy Pratcher, who had been a Victoria Avenue neighbor of Trait and her children, told veteran Buffalo Courier-Express African-American reporter and columnist Henry D. Locke Jr. on July 17, 1978 that Trait had always struck her as being "very concerned" about the welfare of her four children and had always kept them "dressed nicely."

Mrs. Pratcher told Locke the Trait children's "hair was always combed and they always were clean."

"When the mother (Trait) would go someplace she would always take all four of her children with her," Mrs. Pratcher told Locke. "Each Sunday morning the children were sent to church with a minister who picked them up in his automobile," she added.

Mrs. Pratcher told Locke that Trait had gone to bingo with her a few times "but she always seemed unconcerned about whether she won or lost. She appeared to be just passing away time."

The killings, Mrs. Pratcher told Locke, "seems (cq) like a bad dream." She said Trait never bothered anyone on the street and would often just sit on her porch "and read while watching her children play outside."

John Pratcher, Dorothy Pratcher's husband, told Locke that day that Trait "appeared to be a loner. She never really talked to any of the neighbors, even though she stayed across the street for about three years. She just stayed to herself."

Trait had begun studies in January 1978 at the Erie County Community College's City Campus as a liberal arts major specializing in social sciences.

Her courses had included psychology and college sources told Buffalo News reporters Mark Misercola and Lee Coppola a day after the killings that she had sometimes cried openly in class when subjects sensitive to her were discussed.

After moving into the Montana Avenue flat Trait had attended a wedding party with her then-boyfriend, Ernest Hill, a local independent cab driver, the news media learned.

. Because of threatening remarks Trait had allegedly made at that party about her children, Hill reportedly warned her mother to be careful about her, Henry D. Locke Jr. reported on July 18, 1978.

At the July 15 wedding reception, Hill told Trait's mother, Gail had made death threats about her children.

But, Ms. Williams later told authorities she had also attended that July 15 reception and had found her daughter acting normally during the reception. She said she had dismissed the warnings of Hill.

Henry Locke reported that Hill told him he had actually made two unsuccessful efforts on July 16, 1978 to get Gail Trait to open the door to her new flat for him. But Hill said he drove off after the second effort failed.

At about 11:30 p.m. on July 16 as Louise Peterson, owner of 122 Montana and the occupant of the first-floor, later told police that was while she was talking to her next- door neighbor, Lena Jones, she said she thought she heard Trait yell something and then Trait's children began to scream.

Mrs. Peterson told Locke she had initially thought the screams of the children and their crying as they were being murdered was just because their mother "was whipping the kids."

All the women who had been in the downstairs flat during the murders told police afterward that they could also heard Trait, as the knife attacks were apparently about to begin, repeatedly shouting to her children "tell me I'm your mother!!!!"

Mrs. Jones told Locke that when she heard the children hollering she had asked Mrs. Peterson "if I could go upstairs to see what was wrong, because I suspected that something weird was going on the way the children were carrying on."

But she said Mrs. Peterson told her "it was none of my business."

Even so, Mrs. Jones said, she went and rang the doorbell of the Trait flat several times, only to have Gail Trait refuse to open the door for her.

Moments later Mrs. Jones said Gail Trait came out of her flat shoeless and "staggered" down the stairs to the front porch, her hands, arms and clothing covered in blood.

Mrs. Jones later told police that as Gail Trait on the porch had collapsed into her arms she yelled out "you are not my mother -- you are not my mother!"

"I tried to grab her before she fell to the floor." Mrs. Jones told Locke, "But she fell on top of me and got blood all over my clothes. I then yelled to Mrs. Peterson to call the police."

"My conscience is killing me today because if I had gone upstairs when I heard the children crying, I might have been able to save one or two of the children," Mrs. Jones told Locke.

"Those were four beautiful little children," she told Locke. "I can't sleep anymore because I can still see the children.....But at least I know they are gone to heaven," she told the Courier reporter.

Hours after the killings Mrs. Jones told Buffalo News reporter Peter Simon she was sure she would never forget the night she had taken someone's advice reluctantly, only to have four children killed.

Because landlady Petersen had made a 911 emergency call and described Trait stumbling out of her flat in an apparent daze a fire department rescue squad arrived just before police.

As the initial rescuers thought the blood-soaked Gail Trait had been one of the victims of an attack in her flat she was taken, still in an apparent state of shock, to the county's new Erie County Medical Center on Grider Street.

There, she ended up being treated for what hospital medical officials later described as minor cuts.

As police rushed upstairs to the Trait flat they found what one of the Buffalo police detectives who came to the murder scene later that morning and asked not to be identified told the Courier-Express the scenario he found was "the worst thing I've ever seen."

Even the veteran police officers involved in the initial moments after the killings became sick to their stomachs, they later said, with the smell of all the blood in the two rooms where the children's bodies were found.

The initial police officers had been incorrectly warned by Trait's landlady that one of her ex-husbands might still be hiding somewhere in the second-floor flat.

But instead, the officers only found the bodies of the four dead children, Kylia and Demario in the kitchen, with Demario's right leg hacked off at the hip, his right hand cut off at the wrist and both his eyes had been gouged out.

In the living room Amina and Inez were lying dead near the couch, bleeding profusely.

During Trait's December 1979 State Supreme Court murder trial in Buffalo Dr. Judith M. Lehotay, then the Erie County, New York, government's chief medical examiner, testified that despite Demario's dismemberment he may well have actually choked to death on his own vomit.

The vomit found during Demario's autopsy, Lehotay testified, indicated that he may have choked to death, despite having also been stabbed twice in his heart.

"He inhaled his vomit and that alone could have killed him," Lehotay testified.

Amina had been stabbed 63 times and she and Kylia had slash wounds on their forearms and wrists that indicated they had both tried to defend themselves against their mother's rage, police reported. All three girls bleed to death, according to the police.

Of Amina's stab wounds 37 were found in her chest near her heart. But Amina had also suffered stab wounds to the lungs, jugular vein and her aorta, the body's major artery, that could also led to her death, it was determined at her autopsy at the Erie County Medical Center on Grider Street.

Kylia was stabbed 44 times and any of the five knife wounds she suffered in her left lung, which caused her to suffer both internal and external hemorrhages, could have led to her death, her autopsy confirmed.

About six hours or so after the horrific scene was discovered by police and the fire crew, Gail Trait, in a seemly dispassionate manner -- probably due to sedatives she had been given at the hospital -- in a videotaped confession at Buffalo police headquarters told Buffalo Homicide Chief Leo J. Donovan and Detective John K. Ludtka she killed her three daughters and her son to save their souls.

"You probably say it was murder. But it wasn't murder to me. I did it because I was saving their souls," she said.

She initially claimed during that 30-minute-long taped interrogation that "I cut Demario first," but then she corrected herself, saying her first victim was Kylia.

"I think then Demario, then, I don't know if I cut Inez or Amina. Oh, I cut Inez first."

When the detectives asked her if her children had angered her over some incident or incidents, Trait responded "No, I was not angry at them. They had to tell me they were my kids."

Later in the videotaped confession Trait is heard saying "I stabbed all of my girls. I don't know how many times I did, but I remember doing it. I kept stabbing them until they said they were my children."

Trait calmly told the detectives she partially dismembered Demario on the kitchen table.

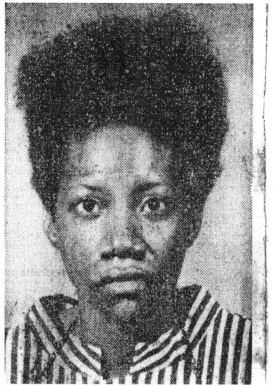

GAIL TRAIT

Though pressed on the point Trait never told the homicide detectives why she felt her four children were not her offspring until they "confessed" to her.

"The only thing I know about these children," Trait is heard during the videotaped confession, "is they were not my children until Sunday when they confessed and I killed them."

Also on the videotaped confession Trait is heard telling the detectives she had not seen her former husband Charles Trait for almost three years. She also said that by the day of the killings, for some reason she never fully explained, she stopped thinking of her own mother, her own maternal grandmother and an uncle as her own relatives.

Several days after the killings, a Buffalo police law enforcement source working on the case told John Pauly, the Buffalo Courier-Express's top investigative reporter that the probe had found that Trait had become angry at her children after several of them told her they had been happy in the county-supplied foster home where they had briefly been living.

That seemed to explain some yelling Montana Avenue neighbors heard coming from the Trait flat before the killings, but that theory was never confirmed by Trait, even after she was placed in a state mental facility decades after the killings.

Trait on May 17, 1978 had turned her children over to the county government's foster care program. She had claimed in a May 9, 1978 affidavit she had signed that she was unable to make adequate provisions for the care, maintenance and supervision of her children because she was then emotionally unable to cope with that responsibility.

In that affidavit she also stressed that her daughter Kylia Person Trait, then 8 and a student at Buffalo's School 61 on Leroy Avenue, had been serving as the babysitter of her three younger children. Also on May 9, 1978 Kylia's father, Joseph Person, and Charles Trait, Gail's estranged husband and the father of her three younger children, signed documents agreeing to the voluntary surrender of the children.

County social service workers took the four children from Gail Trait on May 17, 1978. The county-paid foster mother of the four children, whose name was never made public, had enrolled Kylia and Amina and Inez in Buffalo's School 8 at Masten Avenue and East Utica Street. Kylia entered the third grade at her new school, Amina was a kindergarten student and Inez was enrolled into that school's pre- kindergarten program.

Leo J. Donovan, then the near-legendary chief of the Buffalo Police Department's Homicide Bureau, told Courier-Express investigative reporter John Pauly on July 18, 1978 that he did not fault the Erie County Social Services Department for returning the children to Gail Trait at her request on May 17, 1978.

In May 1978 there were no outward signs of Gail Trail having any type of erratic thinking nor had she exhibited any public displays of mental problems, according to Homicide Chief Donovan. And neither of the two fathers of her children had objected to their return to their mother, Donovan told Pauly.

Noting investigators had heard "some talk" that Gail Trait had been talking about moving with her children to Atlanta, Georgia, where she apparently had friends or relatives and could study nursing, Donovan told Pauly he found no fault with the Erie County Social Services Department's handling of the Trait custody case.

On July 18, 1978 Joseph Person, father of Kylia Told Henry D. Locke Jr. of the Buffalo Courier-Express that before Trait had surrendered the four children for foster care that year a caseworker from the Erie County Department of Social Services, Barbara Murphy, had made him sign papers allowing his daughter to be placed in a foster home. Person said he was told that was necessary because he had been providing financial support to Trait for Kylia.

Person told Locke that caseworker Murphy had told him the four children were being placed in a foster home because officials at the Social Services Department were investigating charges of child abuse or child neglect against Gail Trait.

Person said the caseworker had also told him that placing the children in a foster home would allow Trait to attend college and "to get herself together." Person said he was told by someone in the County Social Services Department that someone had made a complaint against Trait about leaving her children unattended at her Victoria Avenue flat. But Person said he was never told who had lodged that complaint.

Person told Locke he ultimately also agreed to let Trait regain custody of the four children, including Kylia, in July 1978 because by then she was talking about moving with them to Atlanta, Ga. where she had relatives.

Person also told Locke he thought Erie County welfare workers had "acted too hastily" in returning the four children to their mother without spending enough time investigating whether Trait was by July 1978 able to properly care for the children.

On July 17, 1978 after Gail Trait had been hospitalized and treated for what police officials described as superficial scratches she was formally charged with four counts of second-degree murder.

Her formal initial arraignment for the killings was scheduled for July 20. But on July 18 she was initially brought before Buffalo City Court Judge Alois Mazur.

In court she remained silent, not saying her name or answering any of the judge's questions, prompting Judge Mazur to order her held without bail. Mazur also ordered a psychiatric examination.

During that initial court session Trait had just stared straight ahead, remaining silent as the judge asked her "Did you understand anything I said to you? Did you hear me?"

CHAPTER TWO

The System Imploded

According to news media accounts at that time the Buffalo-area public was horrified at the reports of such lovely little children being possibly mutilated by the hands of their own mother.

Less than 48 hours after the killings Fred J. Buscaglia, the head of the Erie County government's Social Services Department — which was delegated with ensure the safety of children in the Buffalo area — and one of his top aides were grilled by county lawmakers.

By July 1978 the Erie County Legislature, the rule- making body in charge of the county, had already been mulling proposals to almost double the size of the county's child protection services operation.

"What was the county's part in this latest and most awful tragedy?" Republican Legislator Marie V. Richardson of the Town of Hamburg, a southern suburb of Buffalo asked Social Services Commissioner Buscaglia and his first deputy, Caroline Daughtry, during a July 18, 1978 meeting of the legislature's Social Services Committee.

Roger I. Blackwell, a Buffalo legislator and one of the most respected spokesmen for the area's African- American community, pressed the two social services officials about whether Ms. Trait had been given any psychiatric assistance prior to the tragedy.

"There was indeed something wrong in that household," Blackwell said.

In describing that polite, but stern, July 18, 1978 confrontation of the two welfare officials Courier- Express reporter M.E. Lindberg wrote about what she called the "brick wall" the legislators found themselves running up against.

"We are not able to discuss the case," Commissioner Buscaglia politely told the lawmakers, Lindberg reported.

"We have been reminded by the state as recently as yesterday about the real restrictions on us," Ms. Daughtry added, according to the Lindberg story.

Ms. Daughtry also spoke during that July 18 session of her department's request to expand the size of its child protection division from 52 to 95 employees and reorganize its operations. She said that had been designed in part to "eliminate the holes" in the protection system.

Republican members of that legislative committee had apparently objected to the proposed expansion of the child protection program due to the extra costs the county's taxpayers would incur.

After the killings Erie County Family Court Judge Victor E. Manz, who had signed the court order turning the Trait children over to the county foster care program in May, opened what had been the routinely sealed Family Court papers on the Trait case at the request of The Buffalo Courier-Express newspaper.

Manz, a product of Buffalo's Black Rock area on the city's north side and a celebrated local judge, ruled that while Family Court papers are normally kept confidential the circumstances of the Trait case justified the public's right to know to way the situation developed.

John Pauly, the Buffalo Courier-Express newspaper's well-known investigative report, disclosed that the court files did not indicate that an investigation of Miss Trait's mental condition had shown there had been any improvement in her condition before the children were returned to her from foster care on July 7.

The court file, Pauly noted in a July 19 article, indicated that in May Trait submitted her children to foster care because she claimed to have been "emotionally unable to cope with this responsibility" at that time.

In an exclusive story on July 20, 1978 Courier-Express investigative reporter John Pauly confirmed that sources close to the fast-moving investigation had told to him the Erie County Social Services Department had done what he described as only a "limited" investigation before returning Trait's children to her.

Pauly also disclosed that law enforcement sources close to the case had told him detectives had found indications that just before the murders Trait had apparently "beat the children until they confessed she was their mother."

The mentally-unbalanced Trait was apparently upset by the time of the killings that her children had indicated to her they had been happy in the foster home in which they had been placed, the sources told Pauly.

"We believe that is what set her off," a law enforcement source told Pauly as the final factor that sparked the knife attacks.

Officials of the county government's Social Services Department did not respond to Pauly's request for answers about whether an investigation of Trait's mental state had been conducted prior to the return of her children to her, Pauly reported.

But Homicide Chief Donovan told Pauly he thought the Social Services Department had checked on Trait's mental condition and found no signs of erratic behavior on her part before her children were returned to her.

"I can't find any fault with their procedures at this point," Donovan told Pauly.

While the veteran homicide detective said he was then sifting through "a pile of papers" on Trait's case he said his own investigation at that point had "uncovered nothing" that would have suggested Trait had emotional problems. He said the police investigation had found that he called "some talk" from Trait associates about her plans to move with her children to Atlanta, Georgia where she apparently had relatives.

Pauly reported that Judge Manz told him that he felt the county government's procedures for dealing with foster care situations and the request of parents to have their children returned to them had to be revised.

"Under the procedure now," the judge told Pauly, "the parents can get the kids back on demand in most cases."

Manz said that under then-current county government procedures "The caseworker (handling a specific child protection case) is supposed to investigate to see if the problem leading to the surrender has been corrected and if so the children are returned without further contact with the court."

"If the Social Services Department finds the problems still exists and objects to the return, a hearing is then held in Family Court to determine the facts," Manz said.

The judge stressed that the Family Court had little involvement in the removal of the Trait children from their mother's home in May and in the return of the children to their mother on July 7. He also acknowledged that before he signed a court order on June 9 giving the Social Services Department legal control of the four children for 12 months they had already been placed in a foster home.

"Perhaps we should consider a procedure where they (the county department) come back (to court) and ask permission before releasing a child" back to his or her birth parent or parents, Manz told Pauly.

Pauly disclosed in his July 19 article that the dry- sounding and highly bureaucrat formal voluntary surrender of children form signed by the biological parents, in part, stated:

"I-we do further agree that I (we) do further agreed that I (we) have been informed of my (our) rights to have the child returned to me (us) at a date, or upon occurrence of a particular event, in accordance with the provisions of this instrument.

"I (we) understand that if a specific date or event is established of the return of the child, he (she) shall be returned by that date or upon the occurrence of that event unless such a return is contrary to a court order entered prior to such date or within 10 days thereafter.

"If I (we) are unable to accept the child upon the agreed date or occurrence of agreed event, I (we) agree that the commissioner of Social Services shall retain the care and custody of the child until such time1 as I (we) notify the commissioner in writing that I (we) are able to accept the child.

"If this consent is for an indefinite period, I (we) understand that upon our written request for the child's return, he (she) shall be returned to me (us) within 20 days unless such return is contrary to a court order entered at any time prior to the expiration of the 20 day period.

"In the event that the commissioner of Social Services fails to return the child within the specified time, I (we) will have a right to seek immediate return of the child in either Family Court or Supreme Court."

Judge Manz said he was in the process of drafting recommendations to restructure the county government's foster-care system and possible prevent tragedies like the killings of the Trait children. The judge stressed that he was hoping to come up with "constructive ideas" that could improve the system of dealing for foster-care issues, including legislative action, changes in the structure of the county's Department of Social Services and the Family Court's dealings with such cases.

Manz said he had been considering such actions for some time and the murders of the Trait children showed the immediate need for such changes.

The judge noted that since Ms. Trait had voluntarily placed her children in the foster-care system when she asked to have them returned to her less than two months later and no evidence of abusive or neglectful treatment of the children by her could be found the Social Services Department returned the children to her without seeking court permission.

The Erie County government had handled hundreds of such voluntary placements of children in that manner through the years but Manz said he felt "there should be some sort of investigation or possibly an examination (of the biological parent or parents)" before such children were returned to their biological parents.

Noting that the county government had been routinely handling such voluntary foster-care cases with caseworkers rarely contesting the returns to biological parents or asking the courts to review the matter, Manz stressed that he was not criticizing the female caseworker who handled the Trait case, just trying to rid the system of its flaws.

Erie County Family Court Judge John J. Honan that same day said he felt the county's child care services should be taken out of the Department of Social Services and handled by a new and independent county government department. Horan said that presently the rights of parents and the social services department were often, in his opinion, given precedence over the rights of troubled children or children coming from troubled homes.

With funeral services for the four Trait children scheduled for the next day, Buffalo Evening News reporter Peter Simon on July 19 disclosed that Mrs. Trait had been allowed to take back her children after telling social workers she was planning to move to the Atlanta, Georgia area with her children to live with an aunt.

Simon disclosed that Erie County social services officials had asked Georgia government officials to inspect the home of the Trait aunt and were told the home was satisfactory and that the Trait aunt said she was willing to help Trait raise her children.

Simon also disclosed that Family Court documents indicated Trait had put her children into the foster-care system that summer because she felt "emotionally unable to cope" with parental responsibilities. Trait had also told government officials that she had been "utilizing her 9-year-old daughter as a babysitter," according the court documents.

Simon contacted Joseph Person, the father of 9- year-old Kylia Person Trait who said he had no indications that Trait had presented a danger to her children. But Person told Simon he felt county government officials may have dealt with the return of the children to their mother "too hastily."

Six days after the Trait children's' funeral the return of the children to their mother sparked a small controversy in one of Buffalo's major civil rights organizations, pitting two officials of that organization — one of whom was a university administrator who had briefly been the foster mother of the Trait children — against the organization's top official.

On July 26, 1978 at a press conference staged right outside the downtown Buffalo office of Fred J. Buscaglia, the Erie County's commissioner of social services, Charley H. Fisher III, president of the BUILD organization, insisted the recent foster mother of the Trait children had recommended to a county caseworker that they not be returned to their mother because she found Ms. Trait to be "mentally unstable."

Fisher told news media representatives at that press conference that Shirley Harrington, who had briefly been the foster mother of the Trait children was a trained social worker herself and had made her recommendation about the Trait children based on what he called her "personal observation of the mother."

Fisher insisted the recommendation of Ms. Harrington, who was a BUILD vice president and assistant director of affirmative action at the New York State University of Buffalo, were made when she still had custody of the Trait children but learned of the decision to return them to their mother.

Fisher insisted Ms. Harrington had told him of her verbal effort to keep the Trait children from their mother and that she said her recommendation "fell on death ears" at the Rath Building in downtown Buffalo, in which held the central offices of the Erie County government were located

During the press conference in front of Commissioner Buscaglia's office in the Rath Building that day Fisher proposed the creation of a local foster- parents review board which would have "the responsibility of determining if parents have met all requirements which will enable the return of their children to a safe and a healthy environment."

Fisher said that panel should consist of social workers, doctors and "people who have been foster parents for a number of years and have demonstrated abilities" in that capacity.

Contacted at her home on Buffalo's East Utica Street that afternoon by Peter Simon for The Buffalo Evening News Ms. Harrington denied making such a complaint to Fisher.

Then a foster parent for a number of children for about a half decade, Ms. Harrington told Simon that she had accepted the decision of county officials to return the Trait children to their mother because those officials were in a position to weigh all the relevant factors in the Trait family situation.

As a foster parent herself, Ms. Harrington told Simon, she had learned that foster parents "don't have a great input" in decisions on the return of children to their biological parents.

Ms. Harrington said county caseworkers had not solicited her opinion about the return of the children and she had not made any recommendations to those officials. Stressing that she was not trained in psychiatry, Ms. Harrington told Simon she did not feel she had the professional expertise to judge the mental stability of Ms. Trait "or anyone else."

She confirmed she had discussed the Trait situation with Charley Fisher after the killings in what she called "general terms," but she said she never made any of the statements Fisher attributed to her at his press conference earlier that day.

On July 27, 1978 Fisher publicly retracted his claims about what he had contended Ms. Harrington had told him about the Trait tragedy, insisting that his comments at the press conference at the Rath Building had been the result of what he called a "misunderstanding" between himself and the slain children's' foster mother.

Fisher admitted that the mix-up was "my mistake." Speaking of Ms. Harrington he said "our signals were crossed. The comments made about her are to be retracted."

CHAPTER THREE

"Jesus, He Will Fix It"

J esus, He will fix it...I know He will fix it," seven boys and girls dressed in white and all about the ages of the older of the Trait children, sang before the small, white caskets of Kylia, 9; Amina, 6; Inez, 4, and Demario, 2, and the hundreds of friends and relatives of the four new angels and their mentally-troubled mother in the sweltering heat of Mount Ararat Baptist Church on Buffalo's Jefferson Avenue the morning of July 20, 1978.

The seven future angels also sang "Trouble in My Way, I Have to Work Sometime" and "If Anybody Asks You Where I'm Going — I'm Going Up A-Yonder to Be With My Lord."

The mourners as a group were urged by the eulogist, the Rev. John H. Peterson, to admire the beauty of the numerous flowers that draped the four small white coffins and he reminded the audience that "the children are not in the caskets. They are with God."

"It is well with my soul," the Rev. Peterson, pastor of Who So Ever Will Baptist Church on Buffalo's

Broadway, said in thanks that the children were already in Heaven.

MOURNERS AT THE FUNERAL

Urging the mourners to "have love in our hearts" the Rev. Peterson said he wanted all of them to ask God "to restore the mother of these four small children and give her the strength she needs to overcome the problems she is facing.

"Death is something that nobody gets used to," the clergyman added. "The children are somewhere in Heaven and if we are determined we will meet them someplace" there someday.

"You must give thanks to God for letting the children live as long as they did. There is a God who cares and we don't know why they had to die, but we will know by and by.

"After a while, it will also be all over for you," Rev. Peterson told the mourners. "There will be no more sick days, no more pain and you will have a home on the other side. If you live right, you will see the four Trait children again and you will ask the Lord how I got over."

Pointing to the four white caskets on the pulpit, the Rev. Peterson said "The children are not in theses caskets this morning. They have put on a new body — a body that knows no pain. If the children could take to me today they would say "Don't worry about it. We're doing all right."

"We must pray for that mother," the Rev.

Peterson said "We as children of the Lord must love in our hearts and ask Jesus to rest (Gail Trait) her and give her the strength she needs."

Asking the congregation to pray to Jesus with him, the Rev. Peterson said to The Lord "You promised us you would wipe away our tears." And turning his head skyward he said "We need a friend this morning." The eulogist also urged all the Trait relatives to be strong.

The Rev. Christine Knox, a friend of the Trait family who had flown in for the services from Chicago where she was pastor of the Christ Universal Temple, reminded the mourners that during their short lives the four Trait children "brought us joy and love and awakened a new, splendid response in each of us and we should rededicate ourselves to greater kindness to all children of God."

The Rev. W.L. Jones, pastor of Mount Ararat, said during the services "The Lord is my shepherd. He is my provider. He is my light in darkness; my strength in weakness and my all and all."

Gail Trait's brother, U.S. Army Sgt. Jace(cq) Williams, asked the mourners to "please do me a favor and pray for these kids' mother" as well as his dead nieces and nephew.

"She simply did not know what she was doing," he said. "Something more powerful than her happened — more than we can understand and more than she could handle."

Gail Trait did not attend the funeral service or the burials of her four children later that same day at the Lakeside Memorial Cemetery in the Buffalo southern suburb of Hamburg. She was under guard that day undergoing psychiatric examinations at the Erie County Medical Center.

The emotions during the church service, on top of the sweltering heat of that morning, caused several mourners to faint.

Outside the church television camera crews were chided by several persons for filming the four small white caskets as they were being carried from the church.

At the cemetery the four caskets were placed side- by-side for burial, with the caskets of Kylia, 9, and Amino, 6, placed on the outside and the caskets of Inez, 4, and Demario, 2, placed between them as if they were being protected by their two older sisters.

Speaking with a cool breeze blowing during the gravesite rights, the Rev. Peterson read from the 22nd chapter of Revelation, the final chapter of the Bible:

"And he showed me a river of the water of life, clear as crystal, coming from the throne of God and of the lamb. And there shall no longer be any night; and they shall have no need of the light of a lamp more the light of the sun because the Lord God shall illumine them. And they shall reign forever and ever."

CHAPTER FOUR

The Legal Journey Begins

On Aug. 3, 1978 Judge Mazur announced that the psychiatric evaluation of Ms. Trait confirmed that she is mentally competent and he ordered her held for a review of her case by an Erie County grand jury.

The judge said Trait had been found mentally competent to assist in her own defense.

That same day Mazur began the preliminary court hearing in the case, which he had delayed pending the completion of the mental examination.

Buffalo Police Homicide Detective John K. Ludtka testified that Ms. Trait had admitted in the interrogation room at police headquarters that she had killed her four children with a butcher knife "to save their souls."

Ludtka said she gave her videotaped confession after her brother and an uncle had left the interrogation room.

ATTORNEY CARL VIZZI

"She stood up and said, I'll tell you what I remember of the killing," Ludtka testified.

The veteran homicide detective said Trait then proceeded to say she had beaten her children for hours and yelled at them repeatedly to call her their mother before she grabbed the butcher knife and began hacking them.

Ludtka testified that before she confessed she had been verbally read her legal rights as a suspect. He said she refused to sign a statement or answer any questions after she blurted out her admissions.

After Ludtka's testimony the judge ruled against a motion to dismiss the criminal charges. That motion had been made by attorneys for the Buffalo Legal Aid Bureau who had been temporarily assigned to represent Trait.

By mid-September 1978 Trait had a court-appointed attorney, Carl Vizzi. Vizzi said on Thursday, Sept. 13, that he would be pressing for her release from the Erie County Holding Center, the downtown Buffalo lockup where she had been kept in the general inmate population because of an alleged failure by prosecutors to launch grand jury proceedings within the legally- required 45 days after her jailing.

Vizzi said that the 45-day period would end Sunday, Sept. 16. He contended prosecutors could not get an indictment before then. He said on Monday, Sept. 17 he would be demanding Ms. Trait's released from custody under the dictates of the state's criminal procedure law on the start of grand jury proceedings.

But on Friday, Sept. 15, 1978, an Erie County grand jury handed up an indictment of Trait on eight counts of second-degree murder in the butcher-knife slayings of her four young children.

During her arraignment that day before State Supreme Court Justice Joseph S. Mattina the suspect complained to the judge that she felt "captured" in the Erie County Holding Center, the downtown Buffalo jail directly across Delaware Avenue from the courthouse.

Than as the judge turned to his court staff to briefly handle some unrelated matters Trait blurted out to no one in particular:

"I want to see my children!"

The judge, who did not hear her remark agreed with the courtroom recommendation of Assistant District Attorney Joseph Burke that Trait be held without bail.

After Vizzi, Trait's court-appointed attorney, entered innocent pleas on her behalf to the eight murder counts he told the judge he planned to use an insanity defense to argue that she could not be held criminally responsible for the murders.

Vizzi told the judge one psychiatrist who examined the woman found she was suffering from mental disease at the time of the crime. He said he planned to have her examined by two more psychiatrists in coming months.

"I have no doubt that all three will agree that my client did not know the nature or consequences of her act or that she was doing wrong," Vizzi said. "The district attorney will have a very difficult time finding psychiatrists who will testify that she was not suffered from mental disease," he also asserted.

Vizzi also complained about her being kept in the general prisoner population at the holding center.   He argued that he Trait could be freed from custody at the jail on bail and that her family had planned to have her voluntarily committed to the Buffalo Psychiatric Center for any needed treatment pending her criminal trial.

Vizzi told the judge Trait's family considers the murders of her four children "the worst possible tragedy that can be imagined" and don't want her released publicly for her own good and safety.

That prompted the judge to say he will have to confer with Erie County Mental Health officials about the best location to keep Trait in custody.

After Prosecutor Burke told the judge the district attorney's office was already legally prepared to go to trial Vizzi objected.

The defense attorney said he planned to have Trait examined in the next month or so by two New York City psychiatrists for a clear ruling on her mental status.

Burke told the judge in response that Trait had already been declared legally competent to stand trial and assist in her own defense by two local court appointed psychiatrists who had just examined her fully.

Justice Mattina handled the indictment arraignment of Trait in his capacity that day as the local judge handling arraignments and other pre-trial proceedings in criminal cases.

When Justice Mattina took up the Trait case the next court day, Sept. 18, 1978 he said he agreed with county mental health officials and ruled she would remain in custody at the holding center. The judge added that she could be transferred to the Erie County Medical Center later if health officials found further treatment was necessary.

Shortly after the indictment Vizzi subpoenaed from the Buffalo Police Homicide Bureau all the "black magic and voodoo items" detectives said had been seized at the scene of the killings.

But during a Sept. 25, 1978 pre-trial proceeding before State Supreme Court Justice Jerome B.E. Wolff the defense attorney withdrew the demand for that evidence. Assistant District Attorney George B. Quinlan Jr., who had been assigned to be the chief trial prosecutor, assured Vizzi that the crucial 911 tape of the call about the grizzly killings would be preserved for his future examination.

At the Sept. 25 court session, which had been scheduled after prosecutors filed a motion seeking to have Vizzi's subpoena for the homicide evidence quashed the defense attorney said his primary consideration in taking that action had been to preserve that 911 tape.

Vizzi told Justice Wolff and Quinlan he was planning prior to the still-unscheduled trial to file a motion demanding all the evidence items he had been seeking from the Homicide Bureau, including a butcher knife and a paring knife his client allegedly used in the killings.

Accusing the Erie County government's Department of Social Services of "grossly negligent" conduct in returning the Trait children to their mother so soon after she had put them in foster care Vizzi in early October 1978 said his jailed client would be filing a $40 million wrongful death lawsuit against the county government.

"These people failed to exercise reasonable care. If they had, these four children would be alive today," he said at a press conference with Trait's mother, Dorothy Williams and other family members present at his downtown office.

"Mrs. Trait has been in and out of hospitals for mental illness," he added. "A medium of investigation would have uncovered her history of psychiatric illness, that she was not emotionally equipped to handle her four children."

Vizzi said he planned to file a notice of claim, the first step in the process of suing a governmental operation in New York State, within the next week in the Erie County Clerk's Office. He said he would name as defendants the Erie County government, its Department of Social Services, Social Services Commissioner Fred J. Buscaglia and other specified employees of that department that he would not identify at the moment.

The lawsuit, he said, would seek $10 million for the "wrongful death" of each of the four Trait children.

Dorothy Williams, Gail Trait's mother and the grandmother of the four slain children, on Oct. 12, 1978 accused the Erie County Social Services Department of fatally imposing on her now-jailed daughter the "Hobson's choice" of either quickly taking back custody of her children before she was emotionally-equipped to properly deal with them or permanently loss the welfare payments that had been cut off when she put them in foster care. Ms. Williams claimed her daughter needed the welfare benefits to survive while she was unemployed and back in school.

Her comments came after attorney Vizzi that day filed a notice of claim against the Erie County government in the

Erie County Clerk's Office and a notice of intent to sue the state government in the State Court of Claims.

Vizzi said he planned to pursue one or the other of the claims. He said he filed both to protect the legal interests of the Trait relatives and his jailed client.

He contended that state or county officials had been negligent in failing to fully check on Ms. Trait's mental state before returning her children to her two weeks before they were killed.

"If they had (made the mental checks), these four children would be alive today," Vizzi told news media representatives.

CHAPTER FIVE

A Pothole in the Legal Journey

As jury selection was about to begin on May 2, 1979 before State Supreme Court Justice Vincent E. Doyle — once one of Western New York's top criminal defense lawyers and a future head of the entire state court system in Western New York — trial prosecutor George B. Quinlan told him his superiors had ordered him not to proceed with the trial because a key prosecution psychiatric witness was not currently available.

It turns out Dr. Syed A. Farooq, a Western New York psychiatrist the prosecution planned to call to the stand to rebut insanity defense claims, had flown back to his native Pakistan over the weekend to deal with his gravely-ill father.

Quinlan told the judge Farooq was expected back in Buffalo by about June 1. He contended the prosecution case would be "seriously prejudiced" if an adjournment is not granted until the return of the "key" witness.

Defense attorney Vizzi strongly took issue with the prosecution request, telling the judge he had just spent two days in New York City rescheduling cases he had there so he could be in Buffalo for the scheduled start of jury selection in the Trait case. The defense attorney also contended he could not guarantee that three psychiatrists he planned to call for the defense would be available if the trial was delayed.

Justice Doyle refused to grant the adjournment, telling Quinlan to start jury selection, noting he knew another psychiatrist who had examined Trait for the court, Dr. Harry Rubenstein, was available to be called to rebut any defense claims. After Rubinstein testified, the judge said he would be prepared to grant a reasonable continuance of the trial, if necessary, to allow prosecutors to call Dr. Farooq to the stand if they still considered his testimony necessary.

Quinlan also argued that the prosecution would be "outgunned" if Vizzi were able to put all three of his psychiatric witnesses on the stand and prosecutors only had Dr. Rubenstein. The prosecutor insisted the trial would be over the mental state of the defendant alone because "questions of fact" about the identity of the killer were not in dispute.

The defense attorney told the judge the prosecution attempt to delay the start of the trial stemmed from what he contended was the fact that they had been unable to find any other psychiatrists "who can find that Mrs. Trait was responsible for her actions." Quinlan then asked the judge for a brief recess so he could go back and talk to his superiors about the status of the case.

When Quinlan returned he told the judge his superiors had ordered him not to proceed with the case. That sparked Vizzi to demand that Quinlan be held in contempt of court.

Vizzi then demanded a dismissal of the charges against his client "for failure to prosecute."

To the surprise of courtroom observers and the shock of the trial prosecutor, the judge granted the defense dismissal motion and ordered Trait committed to the Buffalo Psychiatric Center for up to 60 days of examination.

Justice Doyle told Vizzi he would not sign a document formally dismissing the criminal case until he received assurances from mental hygiene officials at the state psychiatric hospital that the defendant would be placed in either a state or county facility to get the psychiatric care she seems to need.

The judge's order to have Trait sent to the psychiatric center for up to 60 days of examination is exactly what would have taken place had trial began immediately and a jury found her not responsible by reason of mental defect or disease.

Vizzi told the judge that he had been prepared to personally drive her to that Forest Avenue facility for admission.

Later that morning Raymond Kaminski, at the principal officer of the Mental Health Services Division of the state's Rochester-based Fourth Judicial Department told Justice Doyle that Mrs. Trait will have to be examined again by two doctors who could certify that she is need of psychiatric care before she could for formally admitted to the Buffalo facility as a patient.

The judge nonetheless ordered Trait to be taken to the state facility after Dr. Joseph Liebergall of the Erie County government's Forensic Mental Health Services Division, told him the Erie County Medical Center's mental health ward was unsecured, meaning patients sent there could just walk out on their own.

The verbal dismissal order that morning sparked a series of fast moves by prosecutors.

The district attorney's office immediately contacted Justice Michael F. Dillon, presiding justice of the Rochester-based 4th Department Appellate Division of State Supreme Court, seeking to have Doyle's order immediately stayed. The prosecutor's office also immediately filed an appeal Dillon's intermediate-level appellate tribunal contending Doyle's order was improperly granted procedurally.

That day Trait was admitted to the state psychiatric center under a civil commitment under the state's Mental Hygiene Law that Doyle signed. Doyle also ordered officials at the Forest Avenue mental facility to notify him of any effort by Vizzi or any Trait associates to get her released from confinement at that facility. But after only several hours at the psychiatric facility Trait was moved back to the downtown lockup after Justice Dillon issued his temporary stay of the Doyle dismissal order.

Judith Blake Manzella, chief of the district attorney's appeals bureau and one of the district attorney's top legal assistants, publicly that day contended Doyle's civil commitment of the accused child-killer was "totally inadequate for the protection of the community."

But after a May 4, 1978 hearing in Justice Dillon's Buffalo law chambers the appellate judge refused to continue his stay of the Doyle dismissal order.

During that chambers session in the Buffalo City Court Building across the street from the district attorney's office Mrs. Manzella argued that "the brutal and grotesque killings of her four infant children (showed) the capability of the defendant for violence is manifested in the circumstances of the crime."

Manzella stressed to the appellate judge that three of the little children had "suffered 60, 44 and 40 stab" wounds and the eyeballs of the little boy had been gouged out by his mother.

After that chambers session attorney Vizzi came out and insisted his position was that "Justice Dillon has no authority under the law to stay her commitment to the hospital."

"This is a civil commitment," Vizzi said, contending that the appellate judge had abridged his legal authority.

"I told him he should act cautiously and vacate his temporary stay," the attorney added. Vizzi said he was also contemplating a lawsuit against the district attorney's office, the Erie County Sheriff's Office and the Buffalo Psychiatric Center for Trait's return to the downtown jail. He said he would also ask Justice Doyle for a contempt of court order against prosecutors for the alleged mistreatment of his client and her legal rights.

Vizzi said he also intended to file suit accusing the Erie County District Attorney's office of illegally "vengeful, vindictive and cruel" treatment of Trait.

"This is a case for the psychiatrists not the courts," Vizzi said.

Justice Dillon scheduled a May 16 hearing in the custody dispute before the fully appellate court in Rochester.

But late that same day Justice Doyle ordered prosecutor Quinlan and his as-yet-unnamed "superior" to appear before him at 2 p.m. on Monday to determine whether they both should be held in contempt of court. Doyle said he wanted the trial prosecutor to bring with him "his superior who ordered him not to comply with the court's order" to halt the jury selection process.

After the Doyle order was released Quinlan refused to say publicly who his "superior" would be. At that time District Attorney Edward C. Cosgrove was on a 10-day visit to Israel as a guest of the Israeli government.

Karel E. Keuker, who was the chief of Cosgrove's Organized Crime Bureau, was serving as acting district attorney while Cosgrove was in the Middle East.

"My client should be in a hospital getting treatment, not the Holding Center doped up like a Zombie," Vizzi said.

In his contemplated lawsuit over the return of Trait to the downtown jail Vizzi said he was even considering bringing an action against Justice Dillon because he felt the appellate judge "abused his power" by having waited five hours before technically overturning his own order which had vacated the stay of the Doyle ruling he had earlier issued at the request of prosecutors.

The defense attorney accused Dillon of having "flagrantly refused to sign papers" allowing Trait's release from the jail until after prosecutors had put together their arguments why she should be returned to the jail. He said he might try to find another appellate judge to reverse Dillon's latest order and allow Trait to "go to a hospital where she belongs."

The fast-moving legal action on that Friday included with a one-hour closed-door meeting between Doyle and Dillon. After that meeting Justice Doyle's granted prosecutors the right to resubmit the multiple-murder case to another grand jury and he ruled the Erie County Sheriff's Office could keep Trait in custody.

With the Trait family, at Vizzi's urging, already having filed an $80 million lawsuit against a number of public officials and governmental agencies over the allegedly premature return of the four children to their mother who had known mental problems Vizzi said he expected to shortly file a lawsuit against the district attorney's office, the Erie County Sheriff's Office and the Buffalo Psychiatric Center, alleging "malicious prosecution and false arrest" of Trait.

Vizzi, during the May 8 hearing before Doyle, asked that the judge issue contempt of court orders against District Attorney Cosgrove, trial prosecutor Quinlan, Karel F. Keuker, Judith Blake Manzella who was the head of the DA's Appeals Bureau, and Albert M. Ranni, the DA's chief trial assistant.

With the news that day that Ms. Blake Manzella had just been designated to head the Western New York office of the State Attorney General's Office Justice Doyle promptly adjourned the court session for a week, telling all the attorneys he intended to proceed cautiously.

Stressing that he along runs his own courtroom, Doyle said he needed further time amid his very busy schedule of court proceedings in various cases to research the laws on court contempt to determine the extent of his authority and decide what was actually the proper way to proceed in the dispute.

Before the judge adjourned the contempt hearing Ms. Blake Manzella argued that any prosecutor charged with criminal contempt was entitled to see the written charges.

She told Doyle that prosecutors were prepared to formally apologize to the court if their actions were adjudged disrespectful. But she insisted no one in the district attorney's office had any intention of being deliberately contemptuous of the court.

Under state law at that time a criminal contempt charge carried a possible one-year jail term and a $1,000 fine and a civil contempt charge carried a possible jail term of up to 30 days and a $250 fine.

Before court broke on May 8 Justice Doyle said his research would help him determine which type of contempt applied in the Trait case and whether the district attorney's office itself as a legal "person" should be held in contempt.

During a noon-time May 15 session when the contempt proceeding resumed Justice Doyle rejected Vizzi's bid to have prosecutors held in criminal contempt. The judge pointedly said the Trait case had reaffirmed the control of the courtroom by judicial authorities and not prosecutors or defense attorneys.

Doyle ruled after prosecutor Quinlan apologized to him for refusing to proceed with jury selection on May 2. Quinlan told the judge neither he nor anyone in his office who had had consulted about the order to proceed with jury selection had any intent to challenge the authority of the court or to disobey its orders.

The judge said his own legal research had convinced him that he legally could proceed with contempt hearings in the case. But Doyle said he was "frankly fearful that one of the effects of continuing this controversy is that the public will become confused and, in its confusion, have less respect for our justice system."

After that court session Vizzi, visibly upset, said Doyle's refusal to order contempt proceedings was "totally erroneous" and he insisted the public would view the judge's actions as a legal "whitewash."

The defense attorney said he would be quickly petitioning State Supreme Court Justice Theodore S. Kasler, administrative judge for criminal matters in the state's Buffalo-based eight-county Eighth Judicial District to take a look at his contempt effort.

"If an attorney breaks the law, it is no different than if any other citizen breaks the law," Vizzi said outside Doyle's courtroom.

Vizzi also confirmed he had been served with the prosecution papers for the next day's hearing before the Appellate Division of State Supreme Court on the district attorney's office appeal of Doyle's dismissal order.

That afternoon Kasler refused to sign Vizzi's papers seeking a reopening on the contempt proceedings he wanted against prosecutors. Kasler said that since Doyle, who was a judge of concurrent jurisdiction with him, had already ruled on that matter there was no legal need to him to review the issue.

After that day's action in State Supreme Court Vizzi went across Delaware Avenue to the nearby Buffalo City Court Building and filed a Buffalo City Court criminal complaint against Cosgrove and four of his prosecutorial assistants. That Vizzi complaint was given to Buffalo City Court Judge John A. Ramunno who said on May 16 he expected to rule the next day on whether the contempt proceeding which had already been argued in a higher court should proceed and whether he should issue formal summons to the prosecutors.

Ramunno, after he was given Vizzi's criminal complaint late Tuesday, refused to issue arrest warrants against the five prosecutors, which he said

Vizzi had requested. The City Court judge said he had to initially review the transcripts of the State Supreme Court proceedings in the tangled pre-trial procedural battle between the defense attorney and prosecutors.

Ramunno also stressed that "There's a question here in my mind whether he (Vizzi) had a right to initiate a matter of this nature in view of the fact that Justice Doyle already has ruled on it and he's the presiding judge (in the murder case) and he determined there was no contempt."

"Tomorrow I will determine whether I will Issue summonses or, in the alternative, whether I will hold a hearing to determine whether there is probable cause to issue a summons," Ramunno said.

But the next day Ramunno said he had not yet made up his mind about whether to grant Vizzi's request for issuing summonses to the five prosecutors. The judge said "Mr. Vizzi's case is one of the small matters before this court and the court has not yet reached any decision on the matter."

On May 18 Rumanno told Vizzi he would likely rule Monday or Tuesday whether he would issue the summonses the lawyer was seeking against prosecutors. Vizzi insisted he would go ahead with his contempt case against the prosecutors with or without judicial summonses.

Contending he intended to exercise his rights under the law to press the charges Vizzi told the media: "By no means am I going to be precluded from bringing this action."

The attorney said he had followed what he called local procedure in seeking judicial summonses, but if he had to he said he would have his own process servers issue a citizen's summons on each of the prosecutors.

A judicial summons "is not a statutory requirement, this is a policy in Buffalo," he said.

"As a citizen I can make a complaint and they (prosecutors) have to come into court and the courts determine whether there is probable cause to proceed any further. If there is, then there will be a trial," he added.

At that time District Attorney Cosgrove declined to publicly comment on Vizzi's contentions.

On May 16 the five-judge Appellate Division of State Supreme Court in Rochester had reserved decision on a prosecution appeal of Justice Doyle's May 2 dismissal of the Trait murder indictment.

Waiting for both that appellate court's ruling and the City Court judge's impending ruling, Vizzi on May 18 rhetorically asked local news media representatives "Who is the most powerful body in this country? Is it the district attorney's office or the Supreme Court? I always thought it was the Supreme Court. I know in New York (the city where he also practiced law) it is the Supreme Court. There the district attorney would never try to usurp the authority of the Supreme Court. But here they seem to think that they can do it."

Late on Friday, May 18 medical officials and the wife of Dr. Syed A. Farooq disputed Vizzi's claim that the prosecution had "fabricated" excuses to delay the start of the Trait jury trial.

Dr. Farooq's wife, Samina, told this author that day that on April 30 her husband had to abruptly fly to his native Pakistan to assist in the care of his ailing father.

"We couldn't go with him because he had to go suddenly," she said.

A spokesman for the Buffalo Psychiatric Center, where Dr. Farooq was on the staff, told this author that he had received "emergency" permission to take a leave of absence to go care for his father.

Still, Vizzi insisted that by early the next week he would have "documented proof" that prosecutor Quinlan and Dr. Farooq were both guilty of felony offenses. He said he had used a Rochester, New York, detective agency and a New Delhi, India, detective agency to obtain proof Dr. Farooq had traveled to Pakistan merely to begin a long-planned vacation. He claimed his Rochester investigator, who he identified as David Fisher, had used a "ruse" to get Mrs. Farooq to tell him her husband "was on a four-week vacation" and that some of Dr. Farooq's colleagues had confirmed for him the "vacation" claim.

Vizzi also insisted he was in the process of obtaining proof he would show to court officials that Dr. Farooq's father "is alive and well and not in need of medical care."

The defense attorney said he would also be asking the Appellate Division of State Supreme Court to hold off ruling on the prosecution request to overturn Justice Doyle's May 2 dismissal of the Trait indictment "until this new evidence has been introduced into the record."

Countering Vizzi's claims Mrs. Farooq told this author that same day that her father-in-law, a man in his late 70s, had just suffered an apparent heart attack and long suffered from arthritis. She said her husband flew to Pakistan to bring him back to the United States for medical care.

A spokesman at the Buffalo Psychiatric Center, also countering Vizzi's claims to the media, said Dr. Farooq "requested from the president of the medical staff a leave of absence for personal reasons regarding the health of his father. He made a formal request. It was apparently an emergency request."

Tuesday, May 22, City Judge Ramunno formally refused Vizzi's request for arrest warrants or summonses to five prosecutors on contempt of court charges, holding that "the facts alleged in the accusatory instrument (the legal complaint Vizzi filed) fail to satisfy this court that there is reasonable and just grounds and sufficient legal evidence that a criminal offense was committed."

Ramunno also ruled that Vizzi's claims were both "legally questionable" and "factually improbable" given the history of the Trait case.

That ruling prompted Vizzi to say he planned to discuss the Ramunno ruling with Chief City Court Judge H. Buswell Roberts, institute a State Supreme Court show-cause proceeding challenging the validity of the Ramunno ruling and proceed with a City Court contempt case against the prosecutors in the form of a citizen's complaint against them.

Vizzi also said he would continue to try to get a special prosecutor appointed to handle the Trait case to consider the perjury allegations he had raised against prosecutors, calling the dispute a test of the power of prosecutors in Erie County to unduly influence courtroom proceedings.

Late on May 22 Vizzi told Courier-Express investigator reporter Tony Farina that he found Ramunno's ruling to be "a violation of lawful procedure and affected by an error of law." He also told Farina that he believed that judge's action were "arbitrary, capricious and an abuse of his judicial discretion."

At Vizzi's request State Supreme Court Justice Thomas F. McGowan on May 24 granted a show-cause order requiring City Court Judge Ramunno to explain why he should not be legally compelled to grant the defense attorney's request for either arrest warrants or summonses for the five prosecutors.

McGowan signed a so-called ex parte order — a Latin legal term meaning "from (by or for) [the/a] party" without requiring all of the parties to the controversy to be present — scheduling a hearing before him in the higher court's Special Term session for 1:45 p.m. May 29.

In requesting that hearing Vizzi contended Ramunno had improperly given the prosecutors the full benefit of the double on the City Court charges he had lodged against them.

Vizzi also contended Ramunno had used what he termed "convoluted logic" in rejecting his request.

Because Buffalo City Court had recently become part of a newly-reconstituted New York State court system the state attorney general's office would be representing Ramunno at the higher court hearing.

Historically Buffalo City Court judges had been represented in court disputes by the Buffalo Corporation Counsel's Office, the city government's legal department.

In addressing Justice McGowan on his show-cause request Vizzi told him "extreme necessity exists in this case because a complainant (Vizzi) is entitled to his day in court without delay and the public interest would be greatly served by a full airing of the issues in this much publicized case."

"It demands a forum to assure the public that certain individuals are not above the law and must answer to criminal charges just as any other individual," he told McGowan.

Vizzi also told the higher court judge "The public has been left with the impression that public officials in this county are beyond the scrutiny of the law."

After the May 24 State Supreme Court session Vizzi said he was still waiting "documented proof" from private investigators he said he had retained in his effort to get a special prosecutor to consider perjury allegations he had also raised against public officials in the Trait case.

Vizzi's tactics prompted the Buffalo Courier-Express newspaper editorially on May 28 to ask: "Isn't this an unnecessary unseemly side show? Shouldn't the (Bar Association of Erie County) Bar Assn. be taking a look at Vizzi's tactics in this case?"

During a May 29 hearing State Supreme Court Justice Samuel L. Green ruled that the ruling of a City Court judge like Ramunno could not be summarily overturned by the higher courts. Green, the top African- American judge in Western New York and the entire state, held that Ramunno had properly exercised his judicial discretion on May 22 in refusing to issue the summonses or arrest warrants Vizzi sought against five prosecutors.

After arguments by Vizzi and Assistant State Attorney General Douglas S. Cream who was representing the City Court judge, Green told Vizzi he would have to follow the normal procedures of appealing a City Court ruling. That meant he would have to begin at the County Court level rather that at the State Supreme Court level.

During the hearing Cream told the judge Vizzi's continuing attempt to attack the prosecutors seemed to be part of what he called the defense attorney's "apparent scheme to defend his client by publicly vilifying the prosecutorial authorities of Erie County and the entire criminal justice system."

Vizzi countered by arguing that the legal dispute was his way of testing the power of prosecutors in Western New

York to unduly influence courtroom proceedings. He also contended Ramunno had "misread the law" in demanding that he come up with more proof to support his complaints about prosecutorial conduct in the Trait case then was required under then-existing New York State law about how any citizen could initiate lower court criminal proceedings.

The assistant attorney general contended the language Vizzi had used the week before to get a show-cause order in his attack on prosecutors amounted to "a vitriolic attack on Judge Ramunno which itself treads dangerously near the borders of contempt."

"Judge Ramunno has properly exercised the discretion conferred upon him by the Criminal Procedure Law (of New York State) in reviewing the (Vizzi) complaint and holding that it is not legally sufficient and does not provide reasonable caused to believe that a crime has been committed," Cream argued.

"While the district attorney and his staff are entitled to no greater standard of due process than any other person, they are similarly entitled to no less," Cream continued.

Cream contended Vizzi had legally erred in the procedures he used in filling a show-cause motion to try to force the City Court judge to summarily issue summonses for him.

Vizzi, upon leaving court after the hearing before Green, said he would follow that judge's advice and the next day file in Erie County Court a notice of appeal on his continuing attempt to get contempt charges lodged against the prosecutors.

Though Vizzi had to fly to New York City to deal with legal issues involving other clients on May 31 he set the stage for further pre-trial hearings by having his secretary file in Erie County Court the notice of appeal Justice Green had suggested for his contempt of court efforts. That filing gave Vizzi 30 days to submit a detailed explanation of while his contempt case should proceed.

On June 1 the five-judge Appellate Division of State Supreme Court in Rochester unanimously reinstated the Trait murder indictment and severely criticized Doyle for having dismissed it.

The appellate tribunal held that Doyle had "improvidently exercised his discretion" on May 2 when the District Attorney's office refused to immediately proceed with the trial.

In arguments before the Rochester court, John J. De-Franks, the newly-appointed head of the DA's Appeals Bureau, had argued both that Doyle had abused his judicial discretion and that the Doyle verbal court order was a legally insufficient means to deal with the verbal dismissal request the defense attorney had made.

DeFranks had also argued that the Doyle dismissal order had not been granted under provisions of New York State law previously established by the state's higher courts.

The Rochester appellate court, then headed by Michael F. Dillon, a former Erie County district   attorney, ruled that "there is no basis in the record for the trial court's exercise of discretion" in dismissing the eight- count indictment. Doyle, the appellate court held, should have conducted a hearing on the issue of the indictment dismissal request, "given the nature of the crime" and "the lack of showing of substantial prejudice to the defendant and the impact of the dismissal upon public interest."

Erie County District Attorney Edward C. Cosgrove declined comment on all the post-Doyle ruling tactics that defense attorney Vizzi had launched, telling the media simply that his office would "move the matter to trial" as quickly as possible, subject to the availability of Dr. Syed A. Farooq whose absence had sparked the pre-trial controversy.

But Vizzi publicly said the appellate court ruling "has given the prosecutor's office in Erie County more power than it should have." The ruling, he opined, put "the prosecutor in complete control of the courts in Erie County" and "pit the executive against the judiciary."

The legal tug-of-war continued with Vizzi on June 25 sending a letter to the office of counsel to New York Gov. Hugh B. Carey asking for the appointment of a special counsel to investigate what he contended was the misconduct and perjury committed by Erie County prosecutors and the "fabricated" excuse by Dr. Farooq for denying his jailed client her right to a speedy trial.

Vizzi insisted investigators he had hired in both Rochester and New Delhi, India and supplied him with proof Dr. Farooq's trip to his native Pakistan, which caused the delay in the murder trial, had not been unexpected and should not have been allowed to delay the trial.

In mid-August, on the eve of Justice Doyle stepping down as trial judge in the case which was turned over to State Supreme Court Justice Joseph D. Mintz, the Erie County District Attorney's office formally challenged Vizzi's right to both be Trait's attorney in the murder case and also represent the estate of her four dead children in the $80 million civil suit the Trait family had launched against local government agencies and employees in their murders.

In its motion to the court, drafted by prosecutor George B. Quinlan, the prosecutor's office cited a June 7, 1979 ruling by the New York State Court of Appeals, its highest court in Albany, in another case preventing a criminal suspect of claiming on appeal that because the suspect had insisted on keeping the trial defense attorney. In that case, the high court held that an appeal could not be launched on the appellant's claim that the suspect had been denied effective legal counsel at trial.

In one of his last acts from the bench in the Trait case, Doyle on Aug. 15 scheduled a hearing for the following week at which he said he would ask Ms. Trait in court for her views on the lawyer dispute, since she was guaranteed her right under the law to counsel of her choice in the criminal case. He said he also planned to ask her if a legal guardian should be appointed to protect the rights of the estates of her late children.

At the Aug. 15 hearing Vizzi told the judge he considered the prosecution citation of the recent Court of Appeals ruling in another criminal case just a "ploy" to improperly "maneuver" the criminal proceeding in ways that both denied Ms. Trait her right to a speedy trial and get back at him for taking legal action against the district attorney office's handling of the criminal case.

CHAPTER SIX

The First Trial Nears

As the case moved toward jury selection before Justice Mintz on Aug. 22 Vizzi was granted at least a one-week adjournment after he said he needed more time to find out from the governor's legal counsel whether the governor planned to respond to his request or the appointment of a special prosecutor to take over the criminal case from the district attorney's office.

Richard Brown, counsel to Gov. Carey, on Aug. 23 told Marsha Ackermann of the Courier-Express that "The appointment of a special prosecutor to supersede an elected DA is unique and happens only in the most unusual circumstances." Brown stressed that the governor's office of legal counsel was still awaiting a response to the Vizzi accusations from Erie County DA Cosgrove.

Under New York State's executive law the governor could ask the state attorney general to pick a special prosecutor.

On Aug. 29 Justice Mintz, citing what he called a potential conflict of interest in Vizzi's dual representation of Trait and the estates of her dead children, ordered Vizzi to decide which of those cases he would retain. The judge told Vizzi he had three days to make a choice or at 10 a.m. Aug. 31 he would judicially remove Vizzi from the criminal case.

JUSTICE MINTZ

Mintz reminded Vizzi that he had been assigned by the court to represent Trait in the criminal case.

"You were assigned by the court without cost, not only without the consent of the defendant, without any inquiry of the defendant at all as to whether she wanted you or didn't want you" to represent her in the criminal case, the judge told Vizzi

During that court session Gail Trait was called to the stand, but after failing to clearly respond to a number of questions asked of her by prosecutors and her attorney the judge held that it was obvious to him that she could not respond adequately as to whether she understood the issue of the possible legal conflict of interest in having one lawyer representing two possibly opposite sides in a case involving both civil and criminal situations.

But as Vizzi left court on Aug. 29 he insisted he would remain lawyer in both cases, contending he would take a retainer fee from Ernest Hill, who was Gail Trait's common-law husband and father of three of the dead children, and remain the defense attorney in the criminal case.

Contending Justice Mintz had abused his discretion and "was acting outside his authority in seeking to remove me from one of the two case," Vizzi said he was sure his retention agreement with Hill would overcome any conflict problems.

'This is not a ruse to get around an assigned versus retained case," he insisted, contending "Mr. Hill is not paying me my usual fee, but he is paying a substantial fee." He also said if Mintz continued to bar his dual representation he would appeal that issue to the Rochester appellate tribunal.

Vizzi also complained that Gait Trait had been drugged at the Erie County Holding Center hours before the court session with Prolixin, a drug used to treat psychotic disorders. He insisted that was why in court "she could not intelligently answer" questions. He contended Trait needed to undergo a new court- ordered mental competency examination because in court that day he found her "laughing and smiling at the wrong times. Vizzi said he found Trait in a similar allegedly confused state "a lot of time" when he came to see her at the downtown jail because the jail medical staff was only giving her Prolixin once every two weeks instead of the normal daily dosage for that drug.

On Aug. 31 after Vizzi asked Mintz if he could remain the lawyer for the children's' estate controlled by Trait's mother, Dorothy Williams, the judge said no.

That prompted Vizzi to agree to withdraw as counsel in the pending civil suits against the county government and the state government.

The judge also stressed to Vizzi that day that if the civil suits, once filed, were eventually successful Gail Trait would ultimately become a distributor of her mother's estate, even if criminally convicted of the killings, but Vizzi would not be sharing financially in such successful civil actions over the killings of the children.

During the extended pre-trial proceedings in the case Vizzi complained again to Justice Mintz on Oct. 3, 1979 that Trait was then receiving weekly injections of Prolixin, a powerful tranquilizer, at the holding center.

He contested that made her only "synthetically competent" to assist in her own defense and stand trial without mental treatment.

With that the judge ordered a psychiatric examination of Trait to determine the effects that drug had been having on her and what would happen should she be taken off that drug at the downtown lockup.

With Trait at that point slated to stand trial on Oct. 26 Vizzi argued that "It would be extremely prejudicial to her right to a fair trial to have her medicated while in court in front of a jury whether or not she testifies."

And Vizzi stressed that he was still considering putting Trait on the stand before the jury at trial. The trial prosecutor in the case, Senior Assistant District Attorney George B. Quinlan Jr. agreed with Vizzi during that hearing about the issue of the continuing medication of the defendant.

CHAPTER SEVEN

Moving Closer

Hours before Justice Mintz was slated to begin another pre-trial hearing Oct. 26,1979 on the issue of whether Trait was then mentally competent enough to assist in her own trial he pointedly told the attorneys he would not allow the jury trial to degenerate into what he called a name-calling "circus" and he imposed a gag order on all the attorneys.

With the trial set to begin in a week the judge said he was fully prepared to allow the news media full access to all courtroom proceedings. But he pointedly ordered Vizzi to abide by all professional standards of conduct in his dealings with the news media. He stressed that the same order applied to the Erie County District Attorney's Office and all its staff in dealing with the news media until the Trait case was resolved.

The judge said he was issuing the gag order because earlier that morning he heard a WGR radio broadcast and the day before had read a Buffalo Evening News story on Vizzi's contention that Trait had displayed "bizarre behavior" in jail recently and that he found her unfit to stand trial.

The judge told Vizzi that any further comments he made about matters in the case that were not part of the public record of the case could lead to him being charged with contempt of court.

The judge also ordered both sides to refrain from any activity that might be construed, even mistakenly, as an attempt to influence witnesses in the case improperly.

"This trial is going to be tried where it should be tried, in the courtroom," the judge said.

Again the judge told Vizzi that any further statements he made about the case out of the courtroom that might affect the ability of attorneys to select a fair and impartial jury "will not be tolerated."

George B. Quinlan, the senior assistant district attorney who was the chief prosecutor in the case, told the judge he would abide by the gag order. Quinlan also took issue with prior Vizzi comments about prosecutors allegedly making efforts to release information about the case that could show the general public that Trait was guilty. Vizzi had complained about prosecutors allegedly releasing to the news media information a week or so earlier about two men charged in the recent murder of a well-known Buffalo clergyman. He contended that would affect public opinion about Trait's alleged criminal guilt.

Quinlan also denied Vizzi contentions that prosecutors had been harassing, intimidating and improperly influencing members of the Trait family, including her mother, Dorothy

Williams, to try to get them to become prosecution witnesses at the jury trial.

As the mental competency hearing began Oct. 26 both Dr. Harry Rubinstein and Dr. Dadabhal K. Singh, both psychiatrists, testified that during their recent court-ordered examinations of Trait they found her legally competent to stand trial.

Dr. Singh, who examined her four days earlier, testified that he found she would appear normal-looking to a jury and she would be able to both testify and withstand the rigors of strong cross-examination by prosecutors. Singh insisted he was able to conclude Trait's courtroom reactions to testimony and events and her behavior in court would be that of a normal person.

The testimony of the two psychiatrists prompted Vizzi to renew his contention that the injections of tranquilizers into Trait at the downtown lockup made her "synthetically competent."

When the competency hearing resumed Oct. 30 Dr. Jean Jackson, the chief psychiatrist for the Erie County government's Forensic Mental Health Service unit who was treating Trait at the Holding Center, testified that the day Trait was brought to the holding center she actually acted out in a weird pantomime performance the murders of her four children.

Dr. Jackson described seeing Trait kneeling on the floor of the holding Center "telling" her three other young children they were not to bother her while she mutilated her two-year-old son.

During that eerie jailhouse performance Trait "was insisting that the eyes had to come out and the children were not to interfere" with her mutilation of her youngest child, Dr. Jackson testified.

Under questioning from Prosecutor Quinlan, Dr. Jackson said the decision to begin using the powerful anti-psychotic drug Prolixin on Trait in the jail was mutually agreed by her and Dr. Richard Wolin, a psychiatrist defense attorney Vizzi had hired for the defense effort in the case.

Saying she diagnosed Trait as a paranoid schizophrenic whose mental illness had gone into remission because of the drugs she was getting in the jail, Dr. Jackson said she could not predict how Trait would behave during a possibly lengthy jury trial in which the deaths of her four children would be often described to her and the jury.

Dr. Jackson said Trait had been put on a long-term dosage of Prolixin which had been reduced over the past 13 months of her incarceration.

During the hearing Trait, whose weight had ballooned to over 200 pounds during the past 15 months she had been jail — forcing the jail staff to put her on a diet — sat calmly and emotionless during all the psychiatric.

Justice Mintz on Oct. 31 ruled that Trait was legally competent to stand trial. Even though her competency had been induced by the powerful anti-psychotic drug she was getting at the Holding Center, the judge said he found that she was able to understand the proceedings against her.

That prompted Vizzi to tell the judge his ruling "was so wrong that it results in a farce and mockery of justice," adding that he found it "sets back jurisprudence at least 100 years."

With that Mintz immediately removed Vizzi as Trait's court-assigned lawyer and told Vizzi he was to have no further contact with the suspect.

Vizzi then argued for a number of minutes about why he should be allowed to continue to defend the jailed child-murderer. He also told the judge he was voluntarily withdrawing his earlier complaints about the judge's competency ruling.

That seeming apology prompted the judge to reinstate Vizzi as the defense attorney. But he also told him that the "synthetic competency" argument he had been making was the legal equivalent of arguing that aspirin was "synthetically removing the cause of a headache." The judge said he and other judges could not ignore medical progress in the field of mental illness, such as was shown in Trait's normalized behavior after her jailing.

Justice Mintz also said he agreed with Vizzi's claim that Trait's improved behavior in jail was due to the fact that the medication she had been administered there made her "synthetically competent" to stand trial. But the judge also stressed those drugs had been a display of the progress made in the field of mental health which courts could not ignore.

CHAPTER EIGHT

Ever Closer to Trial

After court ended Oct. 31 Vizzi served legal papers on Joe C. Foreman, superintended of the downtown jail where Trait was being held, warning that unless Trait was immediately stopped being administered the injections of the powerful anti-psychotic drug he would be suing the county government.

In a letter Vizzi had gotten Trait to sign, the holding center chief was informed that she wanted to be transferred to a hospital after being taken off the drug injections.

That prompted Erie County Sheriff Kenneth J. Braun to consult with the County Attorney's office. On Nov. 1 the weekly Prolixin injections were halted but Trait was moved from a jail gallery where she had been held with other female inmates to an isolated cell due to concerns that the halt of medication could make her disruptive and put other female inmates at risk of physical harm.

In the sheriff's discussions with the County Attorney's Office it was agreed that if Trait's non-drug condition deteriorated jail officials could invoke a New York State Corrections Law section authorizing the involuntary mental treatment of a disturbed inmate.

By Nov. 21, at the end of the 14th day of jury selection, with eight men and three women already sworn in, Vizzi told Justice Mintz he intended to ask the Appellate Division of State Supreme Court on Nov. 23 to order a change of venue

Vizzi told the judge he would link his change of venue motion to Mintz's refusal to grant him more peremptory challenges to prospective jurors than the 20 both he and the prosecutors had been granted.

Vizzi also complained about Prosecutor George B. Quinlan Jr.'s challenge to nine out of 10 prospective black jurors.

"I find that to be a form of racism I find intolerable," Vizzi said of the prosecutor's tactics. After Vizzi also contended Quinlan had "taken off every juror with any intelligence," the veteran prosecutor stood up from his chair and said "Your honor, that is pure swill."

The judge agreed with the prosecutor, telling Vizzi he had observed the defense attorney during the weeks of jury selection eliminating a series of college- educated, articulate and intelligent prospective jurors.

With that the judge ordered Vizzi to return to court Friday for a continuation of jury selection. He also ordered the defense attorney and prosecutors not to speak to news media workers waiting for them outside the courtroom.

After Mintz pointedly said "Mr. Vizzi, you be here in court at 9:30 a.m. Friday or you will be in contempt of court," Vizzi responded, "No problem."

On the 15th day of jury selection in the case — one of the longest jury selection processes seen in Western New York in decades— on Nov. 26 the second of the two female alternate jurors was sworn in, joining a jury of nine men and three women selected to hear the case.

Trait's attorney Carl Vizzi continued to complain about what he described as the "poisoned atmosphere for Gail Trait" in Western New York and on Nov. 26 he formally sought a delay of at least 30 days from the Rochester appellate court.

Associate Justice Reid S. Moule of the appellate court on Nov. 27 took up Vizzi's motion, agreeing to let him argue his case before the full appellate court in a week but refusing to grant his request for a 30-day delay while he continued efforts to get the case transferred to New York City. The appellate judge ruled that Vizzi had not established a legally sufficient basis to delay the trial.

Vizzi remained firm in his effort to get the case transferred, complaining about substantial publicity in Western New York in recent weeks about the problems of using an insanity defense and what he called public statements from unnamed "unscrupulous and opportunistic politicians" about efforts to try to change or eliminate such a possible defense.

During the Nov. 27 hearing in Justice Reid's Buffalo law office Vizzi cited statements at recent public hearings about the case of George Fitzsimmons, the only man acquitted of murder in New York State and his later arrest for another murder. He also argued that recent escapes from the Buffalo Psychiatric Center by criminal suspects Dennis Buthy and

David Benefield had promoted in the Buffalo area the "community's fear for mad people escaping from less than maximum security mental facility."

He argued all that publicity would prevent Gail Trait from receive a "fair trial" before Justice Mintz in Buffalo.

After the hearing before Moule, at which Vizzi was opposed by both George B. Quinlan Jr., the trial prosecutor, and John J. DeFranks, chief of the district attorney's Appeal Bureau, Vizzi contended "the reason it too so long to pick this jury is that people couldn't erase their prejudice against the insanity defense."

"We questioned more than 200 people to get this jury," he noted. Vizzi said he still planned to go before the full appellate court in Rochester the next week to press for change of venue and a stay of the impending jury trial.

CHAPTER NINE

The Greatest Horror Man Can Inflict

You will hear perhaps the greater horror man can inflict on another man — a mother killing her four children," Vizzi said in his opening statement to the trial jury hours after the Nov. 27 hearing.

As he began, Vizzi told the jurors their job "will be very, very simple. We have top-notch psychiatrists who will testify that this is the strongest case of mental disease or defect they've ever seen."

Vizzi stressed to the jury there was no question Trait had killed her three daughters and son. He insisted the case would boil down to the question of whether Trait was criminally responsible for her actions.

Noting that the prosecution planned to play for the jury Trait's half-hour-long videotaped murder confession to Buffalo Homicide Chief Leo J. Donovan hours after the killings, Vizzi told the jury they would witness Trait "coolly, calmly and collectedly" describing how she had an anatomy textbook open to guide her as she carried out the killings.

"I was going to show that videotape myself," Vizzi said. His remarks prompted the prosecutor to frequently object and complain that the defense attorney's opening remarks sounded more like closing arguments.

Graphically describing to the jurors the numerous stab wounds and the mutilation of the four little victims' bodies, Vizzi talked about how Trait was known to have practiced voodoo, black magic and even satanic cult ritual.

"Could anyone in her right mind do what she did?," Vizzi. rhetorically asked the jury. "The evidence (of her insanity) will be so overwhelming that you may ask yourselves 'What are we doing here?'

Vizzi also stressed that Trait "is an offspring of a family with a disproportionate amount of mental deficiency, with many relatives in psychiatric institutions."

"Could anyone in her right mind do what she did?," Vizzi asked the jury.

Prosecutor Quinlan, in a brief opening statement, told the jury the first police officers who arrived at Trait's Montana Avenue flat shortly after midnight July 17, 1978 found her outside the flat covered in blood and assumed she had injured herself.

But after Trait had been taken to the hospital the officers went up to her second floor flat where they found her four children, ages 2 to 7, dead, with her youngest, son DeMario, partially dismembered, the prosecutor said. Quinlan said autopsies revealed daughter Amelia had been stabbed 63 times; daughter Inez had been stabbed 60 times and daughter Kylia had been stabbed 44 times.

During the opening statements Trait sat emotionless and hunched over at the defense table displaying no reactions about the nature of her children's injuries.

Buffalo Police Officer Raymond Ciesliewicz, a cartographer who drew a floor plan of Trait's second- floor flat where the bodies of her children were found, was the first prosecution witness called to the stand that day.

He was followed by Detective Nelson DiPasquale who photographed the murder scene and Acting Detective Leo W. Malecki and Detective Sgt. Eugene Weisner of the Buffalo Police Evidence Unit who collected physical evidence at the murder scene, including children's clothing, blood stains in the flat and the two alleged murder weapons, a paring knife and a 12-inch butcher knife.

Cross-examining Malicki, the defense attorney asked the evidence expert if Homicide Chief Donovan asked him to look for any evidence of voodoo at the murder scene and had Donovan spoken to him about Trait's claim to police that she had to kill her children "to save their souls."

After Malecki responded that he had not been advised of any voodoo links to the murders Vizzi, his voice raising, said to the evidence detective: "Didn't you read the headlines in The Buffalo Evening News — 'Voodoo Curse' May Be Linked to 4 Stabbings?"

Prosecutor Quinlan immediately objected. The judge told the jurors to disregard the questions about voodoo and he ordered then stricken from the record.

Homicide Detective John P. Regan testified on Nov. 29 that Charles Trait, the suspect's former husband and father of the three youngest victims, told him after the killings that one of the reasons he abandoned his marriage was because the murder suspect was "popping pills."

Under cross-examination defense attorney Vizzi pressed Regan on whether Charles Trait had said anything to him about black magic or voodoo being a problem in his brief marriage to the suspect.

The detective said Charles Trait mentioned the black arts in references to Gail Trait's family and he did admit the murder suspect's brother, Darryl Williams, had told him the murder suspect had seen a woman about voodoo shortly before the killings of her children.

That prompted Vizzi to ask Regan "What it ever brought to your attention to downplay voodoo because Donovan (the homicide chief) doesn't want this to be a voodoo case?

"No," Regan replied.

When Prosecutor Quinlan got up and asked Detective Regan about Charles Trait's statements to him about voodoo in the suspect's life, the detective said the father of the three youngest victims told him his former wife was not involved in voodoo, but he said other members of her family were.

With that Vizzi got up and noted Charles Trait had also admitted under previous questioning by detectives that he not seen his former wife for a fully year before the murders. Vizzi suggested Gail Trait had become involved in voodoo herself in that time period.

That day Justice admonished Vizzi several times to stop repeating his lines of questioning.

After being admonished about his questioning of Detective Regan, who had brought Gail Trait to police headquarters after she had been examined at the hospital hours after the murders, Vizzi apologized the judge.

"Your honor, if I am a little dramatic, I'm sorry. That's the way I ask questions," Vizzi said.

Bad weather in Buffalo on Friday, Nov. 30 caused a recess in the trial until late on Monday morning, but then conditions in the courtroom turned even chillier.

The situation began to deteriorate that day — Nov. 30 with Vizzi, alleging prosecutorial misconduct, demanded the judge declare a mistrial.

Contending that the prosecutor's office had deliberately suppressed evidence to undermine his insanity-related defense, Vizzi contended physical evidence of Gail Trait's alleged involvement in voodoo, including wax dolls, oils, seeds and candles had either been discarded by police and prosecutors either intentionally or as a result of what he called "gross negligence" in the gathering of evidence at the murder scene.

During the argument on the mistrial request the judge frequently accused Vizzi of making "misstatements" of known facts about the incident.

At one point the judge told the defense attorney, "I will not abide misstatements by you. Let's not editorialize because the press is here."

Vizzi responded "I talk like this all the time" and told the judge "You've been incorrect several times" in rulings from the bench.

During the nearly-hour-long argument over the mistrial motion outside the presence of the jurors who had managed to made it to court that day the judge several times interrupted Vizzi for that he called the attorney's "deliberate misstatements of the facts."

After Vizzi complained about the judge allegedly denying his request of daily transcripts of the trial the judge pointedly said:

"Mr. Vizzi, you lied, you have not told the truth in this courtroom."

Vizzi responded, saying "I'm not going to say what I want to say because you're a State Supreme Court justice, but you just called me a liar."

"I told you before," Mintz answered, "that I didn't care what you said in the courtroom as long as it was based on facts."

The judge insisted he had previously only granted Vizzi the right to daily transcripts once psychiatrists testified. The judge said Vizzi have previously agreed to that.

Mintz reminded the defense attorney that they had previously agreed there was no need for daily transcripts because Vizzi had said he would not contest prosecution evidence linked directly to the four murders.

Vizzi said he had recently changed his trial strategy after rethinking the manner in which police had read Gail Trait her constitutional rights as they took her into custody. He also contended, and the judge again denied, that the previous week the judge had agreed to order daily transcripts.

Vizzi said he would not try to suppress the playing of his client's video-taped "confession" to the jury but would deny its use as prosecution evidence because of what he called the impermissible way detectives had read Trait her legal rights. Contending it may turn out to be his best piece of defense evidence he said he was still considering playing the "confession" as part of his defense case.

"Are you going to apologize?," the judge then asked Vizzi.

"Are you going to apologize for what you called me?." Vizzi answered.

"No," the judge said, "Because mine was based in fact. I believe I said you lied. If you would rather, I'll say you misstated the facts."

Court observers reminded the news media that Vizzi had been similar admonished during court proceedings in Manhattan the previous June during a hearing on a 15-year-old boy he was representing there in another murder case.

Prosecutor Quinlan categorically denied Vizzi's claims and the judge denied the motion, telling Vizzi that there was "not one scintilla of proof that the evidence ever existed or if it existed, was suppressed."

Justice Mintz pointedly told Vizzi that "the only mention of black magic and voodoo in the case has come from your mouth in cross-examination."

Vizzi told the judge he still planned to go to Rochester to ask the Appellate Division of State Supreme Court to delay the trial while he prepares a written motion to have the case transferred to New York City

The judge told Vizzi that if he had a "legal basis" to be in Rochester he had to advise court officials so jurors could be advised not to come to court Monday, the day the defense attorney mentioned.

"If you have no legal basis, I will expect you to be here at 11:30 Monday morning," the judge told Vizzi.

After the court session that day Vizzi told the news media representatives present that he had not made any misstatements of fact and he repeated his contention that the judge, without any agreement from him, had denied him the right to have taxpayer-paid daily transcripts of the entire trial.

Vizzi returned to the trial court Monday, only to see the judge deny his second motion for a mistrial, refuse his demand that the jurors be sequestered for the rest of the trial and refuse to apologize to him.

Vizzi complained to the judge and insisted he had "improperly besmirched my reputation and the integrity of the trial. I am going to demand that you apologize to me for stating I lied to the court."

In response the judge said to Vizzi "You have in fact requested a public apology and you had not received it. Now are you ready for trial?"

In response to Vizzi's renewed demand for a mistrial on the claim that jurors may have read weekend newspaper reports of the judge's accusations against him. With that the judge had each of the jurors polled separately on that issue and none of the 12 jurors or either of the two alternate jurors said they had read newspaper stories about that dispute. Though several jurors admitted that they had seen newspaper headlines about that issue, none said they could even remember the wording of the headlines.

With all the jurors then out of the courtroom Vizzi renewed his complaints, contending that during the Friday mistrial hearing the judge had "argued as a prosecutor" even as the actual trial prosecutor, Quinlan, "did not say a word."

"You in fact lied when you said the only evidence of voodoo was from my mouth," Vizzi complained to the judge. "If there was any lying, it was by your honor." Vizzi also asked the judge if the Trait case was his first jury trial as a judge.

The judge responded only by both accusing Vizzi of "attempting to try this case in a place other than in the courtroom" and telling both sides he was continuing his "gag order" barring either side from discussing trial evidence with news media representatives during the trial.

With the jurors back in the courtroom Homicide Detective John K. Ludtka, one of the first police officers at the scene of the murders, testified that hours after the murder suspect was brought to Police Headquarters after being examined at the hospital she sat with her eyes closed and remained silent when asked to explain what happened to her children.

Ludtka told the jury he told Trait of her legal rights.

He said when he then told her she was under arrest her eyes fluttered and either a muscle or a vein in her neck seemed to twitch when she was asked about   her children.

As Vizzi cross-examined Ludtka the veteran homicide detective testified that when he pressed the suspect on the reasons for her actions against her children "First she said" she had acted "to save their souls, then, to make them her children."

When Ludtka returned to the witness stand Dec. 4 he testified that Trait had denied believing in voodoo when she was questions hours after the killings.

Ludtka also rejected Vizzi's contention that a can that police found on the kitchen stove in the Trait flat after the killings may have contained herbal oils and paper dolls used in voodoo rites.

The homicide detective said the can was a coffee can filled with what looked like cooking grease from several frying pans also found on the stove.

Ludtka told the jury Dorothea Williams, Trait's mother, told police her daughter's boyfriend, Ernest Hill, told her two days before the killings that he feared her daughter had threatened to kill one of her four children. But Ms. Williams said she dismissed that warning from Hill after finding her daughter acting normally at a July 15, 1978 wedding reception they had all attended.

On Dec. 4 the jury was played the videotaped "confession" Gail Trait made about six hours after the murders to Homicide Chief Donovan and Detective Ludtka in the interview room at police headquarters starting about 6:30 a.m. July 17, 1978.

"You would probably say this is murder, but it wasn't murder to me," she is heard telling the homicide detectives, "I did that to help save their souls."

Trait, who had gained about 90 pounds by the time of the jury trial, denied to the detectives hours after the murders that she believed in voodoo or any other religion.

Asked if she had felt under pressure of black magic or voodoo" to carry out the killings in her videotaped "confession," she said no. She also told the detectives that the bowl filled with blood that police had found on her kitchen table after the murders had nothing "to do with a ritual thing."

Asked further by the homicide detectives if she had any religious-related beliefs, she responded, "Yes, I believe in myself."

On the videotaped "confession" Trait talked dispassionately and without any showing of emotions. She told the two detectives she had wanted to be a nurse, which was why she had gone through the process to turn her children over to foster care so she could continue her education.

She told the detectives the children were returned to her about two weeks before the murders.

"I told them to say I was their mother," she said.

Asked if any of her children had tried to stop her from cutting their siblings, she calmly said "No, they all sat there and looked."

She said she had taken her four children to the hospital a day before the incident, but she refused to further explain the need for that trip to the hospital.

When pressed about what she thought was wrong with her children which had warranted trip to the hospital she responded:

"The only thing I knew wrong with those children was they weren't my children until I killed them."

"I cut Demario first," she said, only to correct herself, saying she first cut Kylia.

"I think then Demario, then, I don't know if I cut Inez or Amina. Oh, I cut Inez next."

During that taped "confession" the two detectives could be heard asking Trail if she had been angry at her children before the murders. "No, I am not angry at them," she said. But she insisted she kept stabbing them until they "confessed" to her that she was their mother.

"Those kids weren't mine," she insisted. "After I stabbed them they confessed they were my children.

Then they were my children," she is heard telling the detectives. She said. "They had to tell me they were my kids."

"I stabbed all my girls," she said. "I don't know how many times I did, but I remember doing it. I kept stabbing them until they said they were my children."

She also, emotionlessly, described partially dismembering Demario on her kitchen table.

She did not directly respond to questions about why she did not think the children were hers until their death-bed confessions, saying only: "The only thing I know about these children is they were not my children until Sunday when they confessed and I killed them."

She also insisted to the detective during that "confession" that with the deaths of her children her mother, grandmother and uncle ceased to be her relatives.

"I thought they were my relatives but they no longer are. All I have is the children I stabbed with a knife and made them confess I was their mother. They were my offspring because I saved their souls," she is heard telling the detectives.

She told the detectives she had not seen her former husband, Charles Trait, for about three years before the killings.

During the trial on Dec. 5 Homicide Chief Leo J. Donovan kept denying the defense attorney's contention that he either ignored or, in Vizzi's words, "destroyed" evidence of Trait's alleged of voodoo, frequently prompting the judge to rule against the defense attorney's specific questions.

"Isn't it a fact you either ignored or destroyed evidence because it aided the defense," Vizzi asked the homicide chief.

"No," Donovan responded.

"Are you downplaying voodoo because you believe the defense rests on the voodoo issue?" the defense attorney also asked him.

Again, Donovan calmly responded, "No."

Donovan also denied the defense attorney's suggestion that he had felt an obligation to get a confession and conviction because of the $80 million in civil suits then pending against the state and county governments by Trait's mother.

Over the objection of Prosecutor Quinlan, the judge allowed Vizzi to call defense witness Dr. Richard Wolin to the stand. The judge had been told Dr. Wolin had to fly out of Buffalo the next day for a previously scheduled week-long matter.

Wolin, who had previously diagnosed Trait as a schizo-phrenic, chronic paranoid type, told the trial jury that she was legally insane when she murdered her children.

"A person who was rational, who did not have a mental illness, would not have performed the terrible crimes that oc-curred," testified Wolin, then the president of the American Psychiatry Association's Western New York Chapter.

Wolin insisted the videotaped "confession" Trail made for detectives hours after the murders supported his diagnosis.

"In my opinion, her presentation on the tape was con-sistent with the diagnosis I reached," Wolin testified.

Wolin, who examined Trait several times at the Erie County Holding Center before the trial, told the jury what he found to be Trait's beliefs in voodoo and black magic was not a factor in his mental diagnosis but were symptoms of her mental disorder.

Being the doctor who ordered Trait during his second ex-amination of her on Oct. 27 to receive injections of the potent anti-psychotic drug Prolixin at the downtown lockup, Wolin told the jury that after she was on that medication she said to him:

"I murdered my children. I feel awful. I shouldn't have done it."

During one of his two jailhouse examinations of Trait, Wolin said that just as she had in the videotaped "confession" to police Trait unemotionally described for him the stabbings of her daughters and the partial dismemberment of her son.

Though Trait had denied during her videotaped "confes-sion" a belief in the black arts, during her jailhouse examinations she spoke to Wolin of rituals associated with the practice of voodoo and black magic, he told the jury.

Trait also told Wolin that a day before the murders her mother had criticized her after finding in her kitchen a can filled with herbal oils, he testified. Trail said that can had also contained four paper dolls with the names of her estranged husband, an aunt of hers, the former foster mother of her four children, her boyfriend and a woman Trait said was also dating her boyfriend, he added.

Wolin told the jury Trait told him she had wanted to "work roots" against those named individuals or cast a spell against them because of things they had allegedly done against her.

The night of the killings, Wolin testified, Trait told him she had covered herself with herbal oil, a practice recommended to her by a spiritualist she said she had been seeing.

Wolin told the jury that during one of the jailhouse examinations Trait told him that as she began stabbing her two-year-old son, Demario, one of her daughters called out to her "Are we doing to die and go in the ground?" The psychiatrist testified that Trait also told him that as she was killing her children she had also read to them a passage from the Bible.

Trait will ultimately have to confront her actions in killing her own children in the future, Wolin told the jury.

"I think ultimately Mrs. Trait will have to deal with the events that have occurred and at that time she may become quite suicidal," Wolin testified.

Dr. Justin Uku, Erie County's then-deputy chief medical examiners and the first of the three pathologists who testified

Dec. 7, told the jury that slash wounds he found on the fore-arms and wrists of Kylia, 9, and Amina, 6, were defense wounds.

Telling the jury that the autopsies he conducted on both those girls took over two hours each because of the numbers of wounds they suffered, Dr. Uku said Amina had been stabbed 63 times, 37 of those near her heart. He said any of stabbings she suffered in her heart, lungs, aorta or jugular vein could have been the fatal blow.

Dr. Uku testified that Kylia was stabbed 44 times and died of internal and external hemorrhages and could have died of any of the five wounds inflicted in her left lung. He also denied defense attorney Vizzi's claim to the jury that Trait had practiced cannibalism during the killings. The pathologist said Vizzi was wrong and that no human bite wounds were found during Kylia's autopsy on her right arm.

When Vizzi asked Dr. Uko if a person would "have to be in a psychotic state to inflict the number of wounds" he found on the two daughters, he responded:

"It's not normal behavior."

Dr. Catherine Lloyd, associate county medical examiner, testified that Inez bled to death as a result of the multiple stab wounds she had suffered.

Dr. Judith M. Lehotay, Erie County's chief medical examiner, told the jury that her autopsy on the partially dismembered Demario Trait indicated that despite the severe stab wounds he had suffered, including being stabbed twice in his heart, the little boy may have actually died of fright.

Dr. Lehotay said there were even indications Demario actually chocked to death on his own vomit.

"Smart children, when they are in distress, vomit," she testified. "He inhaled his vomit and that alone could have killed him."

Shortly after Dr. Lehotay left the stand the prosecutor rested his case.

The next day — the ninth day of the trial — Vizzi began his formal defense case, calling State Supreme Court Justice Joseph S. Mattina to the stand. Mattina had presided at Trait's Sept. 15, 1978 indictment arraignment.

"She walked into court, I looked at her, I remember being a little bit concerned about her condition and it stuck in my mind that she was in a bit of a daze," Justice Mattina testified.

Vizzi unsuccessfully pressed Justice Mattina for more details of the arraignment, showing him the Buffalo Evening News accounts of Trait quietly asking "Where are my children?" as the arraignment judge was dealing with other matters on the bench.

Vizzi gave Justice Mattina a copy of that Buffalo Evening News article but the witness said he still could not recall hearing Trait ask to see her children during that court session.

Justice Mattina said he did remember noting that during the September 1978 arraignmentthat Trait was noticeably thinner than she was during the murder trial.

Though Vizzi asked Justice Mattina if he could "categorically" state "you didn't hear Mrs. Trait say that she wants to see her children," Justice Mintz ruled that question improper and Justice Mattina left the witness stand.

That morning Vizzi told the news media outside the court-room that the case against Trait, in his opinion, "requires an analytical mind and I'm afraid to trust this particular group of people that we have on the jury with my client's life."

Vizzi then called to the stand Kimberly Oswald, a social worker with the Erie County Forensic Health Service, who attended the initial arraignment of Trait in Buffalo City Court on July 17, 1978.

"She just stood there and stared and blinked and that was all she did," Oswald testified about that court session. She also told the jury Trait had to be escorted by a court official to stand before City Judge Alois Mazur when he called for her arraignment. Trait did not respond to any of that judge's questions and she ended up being placed in a psychiatric lockup ward at the Erie County Holding Center across the street from the City Court building that day, the social worker testified.

When the trial resumed on Monday, Dec. 10 Vizzi complained to Justice Mintz before the jury about news media reports on the third escape from a state mental facility by Dennis Buthy, a notorious Buffalo mental patient.

Buthy, then 35, had been acquitted in 1972 by reason of insanity on criminal charges in the brutal 1967 knifing and meat cleaver attack on a 19-year-old female elevator operator in a downtown Buffalo building.

After Vizzi insisted the Buthy news reports further "poisoned" the atmosphere against the insanity defense in Western New York courts, Justice Mintz called each of the jurors into his chambers individually to see how much each had been exposed to those news accounts.

After the judge said he was satisfied that the Buthy escape had not tainted the Trait jurors Vizzi called this author, then a Buffalo Evening News reporter, to the stand to testify about the Sept. 15, 1978 murder arraignment before Justice Mattina.

Seated about 10 feet behind Trait as she was standing at a defense table before Justice Mattina, then turned to a court clerk discussing scheduling of other cases, the author testified that Trait randomly, and to no one in particular, "blurted out words to the effect that she wanted to see her children" adding that "was a rather peculiar thing to say" so soon after she had murdered her four children.

The author also testified that during that September 1978 murder arraignment Trait "looked more bewildered than anything else."

That afternoon Dr. Jean Jackson, the chief psychiatrist of the Erie County Forensic Mental Health Service, testified that on Trait's first day in custody at the Erie County Holding Center she was seen acting out the stabbings of her children as she sat on the floor of the women's gallery at that downtown lockup.

Dr. Jackson testified that when she first saw Trait at the holding center she was sitting in a trance-like state in that gallery.

"She was extremely agitated and I observed her going through a reenactment of the crime. She was in an acute psychotic condition," Dr. Jackson testified. "I consider she was suffering from psychosis and appeared suicidal.

Dr. Jackson told the jury she prescribed anti- psychotic drugs for Trait that day as Trait kept talking about her children, apparently unaware she had killed all of them hours earlier.

"She was concerned for their welfare and said her mother was caring for them," she continued.

Dr. Jackson said the defendant's behavior prompted her to order her hospitalization out of fears that she was then suicidal.

Dr. Jackson told the juror her opinion about Trait that day had not been based in anyway about the impending court proceedings in the case but solely to determine her course of treatment of the suspect.

The trial came to a very brief halt on Dec. 11 after Jerry M. Soloman, a colleague of the trial prosecutor, and defense attorney Thomas M. Daley began laughing as they talked in the courtroom about another case assigned to Justice Mintz. Solomon later told news media representatives neither he nor Daley had been laughing at Vizzi in the courtroom.

Vizzi, having mistaken their laughter as being aimed at him, had asked Justice Mintz to quiet "these clowns here who are smiling, who can't conduct themselves in a professional manner."

After Vizzi then insisted he could call almost a dozen persons into the courtroom to laugh about some of Prosecutor Quinlan's questions Justice Mintz angrily stopped him from talking.

"I warn you," Justice Mintz told Vizzi from the bench, "that your conduct is close to and maybe contemptuous."

The judge angrily told Vizzi that he knew Solomon and Daley had come to court and were "talking about a case assigned to this court."

As Vizzi continued to complain Justice Mintz again warned him his conduct was bordering on contempt of court and he admonished him about interrupting the prosecutor's questioning of witnesses.

"We're going to operate with proper courtroom decorum," Justice Mintz told Vizzi. "I've permitted it enough and it's not going to continue," the judge said of Vizzi's verbal complaints before the jurors.

Later that day Dr. John M. Wadsworth, a psychiatrist who examined Trait three times after the murders, told the jury he found her shielding herself from thoughts of having murdered her own children by referring to them during his interviews as fish, birds and paper dolls.

Calling Trait a victim of paranoid schizophrenia, Wadsworth testified that she was not criminally responsible for the killings.

Dr. Wadsworth said he based his evaluation of Trait on the jailhouse interviews he had with her July 23, 1978, less than a week after the killings and on Aug. 2, 1978 and Feb. 3, 1979.

The psychiatrist told the jury he found Trait to be of average or above average intelligence. He said she told him she had been suffering hallucinations after the killings and she described what he called "a ritual quality" to the killings.

"She described having watched the Hardy Boys television program and described how, in a bland, affectless (unfeeling) way that she went into the kitchen and started murdering her children," Dr. Wadsworth testified.

For weeks before the killings Trait had, according to reports Dr. Wadsworth said he reviewed, displayed signs of ambivalence toward her children and bizarre actions and thoughts and a preoccupation with voodoo.

Reports of Trait displaying anxiousness and distance to loved ones and friends and possibly suffering from hallucinations and delusions were all signs of her psychosis prior to the killings, Dr.

Wadsworth testified.

As prosecutor Quinlan cross-examined Dr. Wadsworth he contended it was possible that Trait killed her children because she was angry that her family had stopped an aunt from coming to Buffalo on the weekend of July 15, 1978 at her request to take her four children back with her to Atlanta, Georgia.

Raising that theory for the first time as a possible motive for the killings, Quinlan suggested that anger with her family is why Trait had not attended a wedding with her mother and other family members that weekend.

Dr. Wadsworth testified that Trait never mentioned such a situation to him as he talked to her in jail, but he agreed with the prosecutor that even mentally ill individuals can be mentally aware of criminal activity as they are committing such actions.

Jace (cq) Williams, Trait's half-brother, was called to the witness stand by Vizzi on Dec. 13. Williams told the jury that mental illness was prevalent on his half- sister's side of the family. He said he had noticed Trait acting peculiar some two weeks before the killings of her children.

As Trait quietly smiled as she sat at the defense table, Williams told the jury his half-sister had one uncle they called "Bozo" and a grandmother they bought knew as the "Rag Lady."

Williams said he saw Trait while he was home on leave from the U.S. Army in May and June 1978. He told the jury he felt very close to his half-sister and was upset on learning she had given up her four children to foster care so she could go back to school to study for a nursing degree.

Williams said when he was home on leave in mid-1978 he found Trait overly afraid of something, frequently reading the bible and putting pepper in her shoes for some inexplicable reason.

Trait's half-brother also told the jury that in the summer of 1978 he found her continually burning oil of some sort in a coffee can on the stove of her flat in a low flame. He said he also saw in her flat packets of seeds that defense attorney Vizzi, over the prosecutor's objections, characterized as a sign of her love of voodoo.

Williams testified about the mental illness among Trait's relatives over the objections of the prosecutor.

The next morning, Dec. 14, one of the female jurors was seen visibly shuddering as the jurors were shown two dozen black and white photographs of the mutilated bodies of the four young victims as Vizzi rested the defense case.

Vizzi had earlier objected to the proposed showing of what he described as the "grisly" photos to the jurors but reversed his opinion, telling the judge he might have the jurors look at color photos of corpses before they begin deliberations. Justice Mintz agreed to Vizzi subpoenaing color photos but reserved decision on whether he would let the jurors look that those photos.

After Vizzi rested his case that morning Prosecutor Quinlan began his rebuttal case by calling to the stand Marsha Kruzynski, an Erie County sheriff's deputy at the Erie County Holding Center who had been observing Trait for that past 17 months.

Kruzynski — who was not cross-examined by Vizzi — testified that she found Trait acting rationally for the past 17 months in the downtown jail. She also told the jury that a week after the four children were killed Trait told her during a jailhouse conversation that she knew what she was doing during that slaughter.

Dr. Harry Rubenstein, a psychiatrist called to the witness stand by the prosecutor on Monday, Dec. 17, 1978, told the jury he found Trait to be suffering from an anti-social personality disorder and that she should be found criminally liable for the murders.

A court-appointed mental health expert assigned to the Trait case, Dr. Rubenstein said that he found no basis for diagnosing Trait a paranoid schizophrenic based on his two jailhouse examinations of her and a review of her videotaped "confession," and his review of her background.

Dr. Rubenstein told the jury he found Trait came from a family where little love was shown by each family member to each other. He said she grew up seeking gratification from other persons and through her use of drugs and alcohol.

Talks with Trait at the downtown holding center, Dr. Rubenstein said, convinced him she considered her children a burden. He said she apparently was prompted to kill them in anger after her relatives had stopped an aunt from taking them back to Atlanta, Georgia so she could go back to school for nurse studies.

"She could have taken her anger out on the kids," Dr. Rubenstein testified. He insisted the multiple stab wounds she inflicted on them were not inconsistent with at the actions of an anti-social personality disorder.

Dr. Rubenstein also told the jury that reports of Trait acting out the killings at the downtown jail hours after the killings was not necessarily the result of her suffering symptoms of mental disease.

"She knew what she was doing," Dr. Rubenstein told the jury. He said she knew the nature and consequences of her actions and knew that her conduct was wrong.

In cross-examining Dr. Rubenstein, the defense attorney showed him a color photograph of the gruesome murder scene, saying to him "Are you suggesting this was done by a sociopath?"

"It can be," Dr. Rubenstein responded. Refusing to change his diagnosis when Vizzi asked him if her stabbing of her three daughters some 66 times and partially dismembering her son were signs of her "anger," he responded:

"I can't give you an exact answer why, but I can tell you, according to the literature that sociopaths, when they murder, usually mutilate."

Trait lived the first 27 years of her life for herself, Dr. Syed A. Farooq, a second prosecution psychiatrist, testified on Dec. 18.

Agreeing with Dr. Rubenstein that Trait has an anti- social personality and killed her children to "spite" her family who had stopped her from turning over the children to an aunt living in Georgia so she could continue her schooling, Dr. Farooq testified that "she was existing for no purpose" except "to have fun for the moment."

Dr. Farooq told the jury that during one of his three jailhouse examinations of Trait she told him she had married her husband "to spite" a boyfriend who had jilted her for another woman. She told him during another jailhouse session that once she had thrown a dog out a window of her second-floor apartment because she was mad at a boyfriend, he testified.

"She was so preoccupied with herself, she didn't even care for her children" and based on reports of her heavy use of drugs and alcohol and neglect of her children Trait was following what psychiatrists call the "pleasure-pain principle — seeking pleasure and avoiding pain," he testified.

During their jailhouse sessions Dr. Farooq said Trait's apparently vivid memory of how her children had died and her failing to show any emotion as she recalled their deaths convinced him she was not suffering from mental illness at the time of the killings,

Her homicidal actions were indicative of the anti- social personality she has had throughout her life, Dr. Farooq testified.

That afternoon Justice Mintz dismissed four counts of second-degree murder that were based on contentions Trait's actions were reckless. Over objections of Vizzi he ruled the jury will consider four other counts of second-degree murder that alleged Trait intentionally killed all four children.

"How could a mother in her right mind do this to her babies? Is there any way anger, hostility or spite could make her do that?" Vizzi asked the jury in his Dec. 19 closing argument.

Pressing for the jury to find Trait not criminal responsible by reason of mental disease or defect, Vizzi repeated all the details of each of the killings, telling the jury "How often do you hear about a mother doing what Gail Trait did?"

He told the jury to reject as self-serving and fabrications the claims of the two prosecution psychiatrists that Trail was not mentally ill and only had an anti-social personality and likely killed her children in a fit of anger.

In an unusual development Prosecutor George B. Quinlan interrupted Vizzi's closing arguments almost 70 times, with the judge agreeing with the prosecutor's complaints on 36 of those objections.

Vizzi told the jury to consider the findings of mental illness expressed by the two defense psychiatrists. He also urged the panel to examine the color photos of the murder scene. And he asked the jurors not to make their deliberations a game of "two against two (psychiatrists)."

The prosecutor pointedly called for Trait's conviction, citing the murder scene evidence and agreeing with Vizzi that the jury should review the color photos of all four murders children.

Quinlan stressed to the jurors that Trait was not the psychotic woman Vizzi tried to show.

Trait's videotaped "confession" hours after the killings showed she was in touch with reality during the fatal incident, Quinlan argued.

Quinlan told the jurors Trait's effort to show she suffered mental illness and her alleged voodoo connections were things the she made up after the slayings.

The woman seen on that videotape was "an angry, frustrated woman...but not a psychotic," Quinlan argued.

The jury of nine men and three women got the case about 5 p.m. Dec. 19 after the judge told them they were not allowed to let sympathy for Mrs. Trait or her children interfere with their ultimate verdict.

After being taken to supper the jurors spent about three and one-half hours in actual deliberations until about 10:45 p.m. before being sequestered in a downtown hotel.

Deliberations resumed about 9 a.m. Dec. 20 with the jurors having a court stenographer reread for them the testimony of prosecution psychiatrist Syed A. Farooq and defense psychiatrist Richard Wolin.

The jurors viewed the videotaped "confession" during their deliberations Wednesday night and again late on the afternoon of Dec. 20.

Just before the jurors were to be taken to dinner on Dec. 20, the foreman passed a note to the court clerk reporting that a verdict had been reached.

At 5:55 p.m. the foreman of the jury said only "guilty" as the court clerk asked him for the findings on each of the four counts of second-degree murder involved in the deliberations.

Several of the women and even male jurors had tears in their eyes as the court clerk then polled them to ensure the verdict was unanimous.

Listening to the verdict which rejected the insanity defense, Trait stood expressionless, showing no emotions. She remained stone-faced as she was lead out of the courtroom by Sheriff Deputy Leona Fitzgerald after the judge scheduled her to be sentenced on Jan. 25, 1980.

Afterward Vizzi told news media representatives "I can't believe it. I'm in a state of shock," vowing to have the conviction appealed to the Appellate Division of State Supreme Court in Rochester.

Vizzi vowed to win a reversal of the conviction and seek to have the case transferred for a retrial in New York City, saying "the insanity defense is alive and well in New York City" in contrast to what he called the "poisoned" atmosphere about the insanity defense in the Buffalo area.

When asked by reporters why he agreed to have the case tried before a jury rather than have a bench trial with a judge deciding the verdict, Vizzi said:

"When I said the atmosphere was poisoned against the insanity defense in Erie County I wasn't limiting it to jurors. I meant judges as well."

Vizzi said he would, as part of his planned appeal, show possible exposure of jurors to news stories during the trial about the escape of Dennis Buthy from the Gowanda Psychiatric Center south of Buffalo where he was undergoing treatment after his not guilty by reason of insanity verdict in an earlier Buffalo crime.

Prosecutor Quinlan declined to comment to the news media as he left the courtroom.

As the jurors left the courtroom most declined to talk to new media representatives. But one of the male jurors, asking that his name not be disclosed, said the panel had a "tough time" reaching a guilty verdict.

"All I can say is I hope I don't have to do it again," the male juror said as he left the court house of his work on the jury.

CHAPTER TEN

The Public Reacts

Because the four Trait children had been literally butchered by their mother the New York State Senate's Select Committee on Child Abuse criticized the Erie County government's Department of Social Services for returning children to their parents without adequate investigations.

In a direct reference to the Trait case — without mentioning Trait by name — the Senate committee criticized the county department for returning children to their parents from foster care after parents learned they would lose welfare benefits with their children in foster care.

Three days after the guilty verdict Henry D. Locke Jr., the Buffalo Courier-Express' much-honored African- American columnist, wrote that "Many members in the black community are up in arms in the wake of the conviction of Gail Trait for murdering her four small children."

Locke's column stressed that "Many dispute the jury verdict, saying Mrs. Trait is obviously mentally ill and should have been found innocent by reason of insanity. And some feel Mrs. Trait should not have stood trial at all until she had received additional psychiatric treatment to make her more capable of defending herself."

Locke's column cited an African-American who was an official at Buffalo State College and who asked that her name not be published as she said of the verdict:

"If she had been white, she would have been declared criminally insane and placed in an institution where she could get proper medical attention. But because she was black and poor, the court decided that she should stand trial for the crime. The bad thing about the trial was that the jury found a sick woman guilty of murder. That never should have happened."

That Buffalo State official also said during her interview by Locke: "Black women may do a few bad things. But they don't go around butchering their children. It is beyond my imagination how a jury could find her guilty, saying she was sane at the time of the crime."

In his Dec. 23, 1979 column Locke cited complaints from the African-American professional community that only one black person served on the Trait jury. Locke also cited the successful efforts of prosecutors during jury selection to use their permitted "peremptory" challenges to eliminate 13 of the 14 black persons who were in the jury pool for the Trait murder trial.

Locke noted each side during the jury selection process had been allowed to eliminate up to 20 prospective jurors through peremptory challenges without having to explain the reasons why that wanted that person eliminated from the possible jury.

Locke's Dec. 23 column cited the following complaint about the Trait case made by Allison Hedgepeth, vice president of the University of Buffalo College Chapter of the National Association for the Advancement of Colored People (NAACP):

"Sending Mrs. Trait to jail will not serve any useful purpose. She needs medical attention, the type she can receive in a mental institution. She will not get that attention in a crowded jail cell.

"I believe she was found guilty because the jurors wanted to make people think black people are evil. The trial was politically motivated because someone made a decision that Mrs. Trait had to be convicted," Hedgepeth also told Locke.

Locke noted in his Dec. 23 column that some unidentified members of the Buffalo community he had talked to about the Trait case "suggested that the jurors may have assumed that they were trying Vizzi, because of the many clashes he had with State Supreme Court Justice Joseph D. Mintz during the trial."

In that column Locke quoted a female teacher at the Campus West School at Buffalo State College who asked that her name not be published because she feared she would be criticized by public school officials.

That female teacher told Locke she found fault with the Erie County District Attorney's office for even forcing Mrs. Trait to stand trial, stressing that that she also felt that many white persons who were obviously sick before going to trial were found innocent by reasons of insanity after the trial.

That black woman cited Buffalo's George Fitzsimmons who killed his parents and Dennis Buthy who attacked a female Buffalo elevator operator with a meat clever, yet both were both found not guilty by reason of mental disease or defect.

"I have no doubt in my mind," that Campus School teacher told Locke, "that if Mrs. Trait had been white she would have been found innocent by reason of insanity."

Locke ended his Dec. 23 column by noting that a number of unidentified white professionals he had talked with about the Trait case "lashed out at the trial, saying Mrs. Trait never should have been tried. Those unidentified white professionals told Locke the trial was an injustice in a system which is supposed to be democratic. Those professionals called the prosecution decision unfair and that Ms. Trait never should have gone on trial, Locke wrote.

As a result of his Dec. 23 column Locke was contacted by a number of leaders of the local black community including, he explained in a Dec. 24 story, a mental hygiene professional, a retired education, an elected official and civil rights leaders.

They all criticized the district attorney's office and the county government's Social Services Department for the manner in which the Trait situation was handled, Locke reported.

Locke said Erie County District Attorney Edward C. Cosgrove declined to comment when contacted on Dec. 23 and

Fred J. Buscaglia, the social services commissioner, could not be contacted for comment.

Dr. Ellen E. Grant, the in-care coordinator at the Buffalo Psychiatric Center, was quoted by Locke saying Trait should be sent to a hospital for mental services that jailing will prevent her from receiving.

Locke reported Dr. Grant suggested county welfare officials may have erred in returning Trait's children to her from the foster home where they had been placed. She also criticized the mental evaluation of Trait, suggesting Trait may not have been fit to stand trial.

"If she was sane or insane," Dr. Grant told Locke, "she still is not going to receive the help she needs in jail."

Erie County Legislator Minnie Gillette told Locke she felt the county welfare agency (the Social Services Department) was not blameless in the Trait case.

Gillette also criticized the jurors, saying:

"It was no way humanly possible one person can kill and mutilate four people without being insane.

"When you look at George Fitzsimmons and Dennis Buthy, both white and both put in mental institutions after brutal crimes because they were suffering from mental strains, then one must conclude that Mrs. Trait is facing a jail term because she is black and poor."

Mrs. Jessie Blackman, a retired Buffalo educator active in civil rights affairs, was quoted by Locke as contending someone in the county government's welfare administration "fell down on the job" in returning the children to their mother.

Ms. Blackman also criticized the makeup of the trial jury, saying "the jury system in Erie County has never been fair in dealing with minorities." She told Locke she doubted any jurors selected in Erie County could have been impartial in the case.

Lelia F. Byrd, a direct service coordinator for the Erie County Department of Mental Health, blamed American society and the county government's welfare operation for allowing the Trait tragedy.

Mrs. Byrd told Locke a better investigation should have been conducted before the children were returned to Trait because when a person is poor and hungry and on welfare her benefits were only increased with the children in the home.

Raphael DuBard, a former New York State president of the National Association for the Advancement of Colored People (NAACP), told Locke:

"It is highly improper for a jury to think a woman could commit such a crime." DuBard told Locke he felt Trait "had to be in a trance or stupor when the children were murdered. A rational, thinking person could not have done that."

Locke also quoted Rosetta Moultrie, a former president of the Kenfield-Langfield Tenant Association, who told him she felt the "minds of the jurors were poisoned against her (Trait) before the trial." She also told Locke she felt a retrial in the case should be held in New York City

Morris Aiken, a spokesman for the Buffalo chapter of Operation PUSH (People United to Save Humanity), issued a statement for his civil rights organization highly critical of the

Trait conviction. Aiken insisted Trait had been convicted because she was poor.

As Christmas 1979 approached Locke managed to contact
Adam Jones, the lone black juror at the trial, and a white
woman who was a member of the jury for the first five days
of the trial and then got permission from Justice Mintz to be
relieved of duty.

That former female juror, who talked to Locke after he
agreed not to disclose her identify, stressed to Locke that she
periodically came to the courtroom for the rest of the trial.

Jones told Locke he was the last holdout on the jury for a
guilty verdict, but he decided to make the guilty verdict unanimous because to him, Trait "did not show any remorse"
when she explained to police in the videotaped "confession"
how her children were killed.

"I believed she was guilty," Jones told Locke, "But I could
have hung (causing a deadlocked jury) the jury. I asked for
the videotape of the proceedings (Trait's police interrogation)
to be relayed before I made my decision."

Jones told Locke that he and another juror held out the
longest on the verdict, but he changed his mind when he became that last holdout. But Jones stressed that none of the
other jurors had pressured him to change his vote.

"So I finally concluded that anyone who could remember
all the details of how she stabbed one of her children in the
heart and cut off his hand meant she could not have been insane," Jones said.

The former white woman juror told Locke that before testimony began she had been sure Trait was not in her right

mind when she killed her children, saying "no mother in her right mind could have committed such a crime."

That woman told Locke that several times during the trial she saw Adams Jones and another of the jurors dozing off, with sheriff deputies having to awaken them.

Jones spoke to Locke about that, insisting he had not fallen asleep during any of the testimony, but had "nodded" a couple of times, prompting a sheriff's deputy to shake him.

The while woman who had been excused from the jury spoke critically to Locke about Justice Mintz' behavior at various times during the trial.

The woman insisted that several times as defense attorney Vizzi was questioning witnesses on the stand she could see the judge holding his hands over his face, something she said she never saw the judge do when the prosecutor had the floor.

On Christmas Day,1979 Theodore Kirkland, a commissioner of the New York State Parole Board and a noted Buffalo civil rights advocate, told Locke he was sharply critical of the jury selection process in the Trait case.

Kirkland, then on leave of absence from his career as a Buffalo police officer, told Vizzi he felt that Trait would have been found innocent by reason of insanity if more than just one black person had been on the trial jury.

Kirkland insisted Trait had not been tried by a jury of her peers.

Locke reported that of the more than 100 persons he talked to about the Trait verdict many agreed that the jury selection process in the Buffalo courts should be changed to make it more likely that a criminal is tried by a panel of his or her real peers.

Kirkland told Locke he agreed with that sentiment, saying "what I'm advocating is that when a person is tried, he should be tried by his peers."

Stressing that he was not suggesting that when blacks commit crimes they should not be punished, Kirkland told Locke "It is time for black leaders to start demanding cures for discriminatory policies and especially in the criminal justice system where the black community is losing many of its youths because of jurors who are insensitive to the cultural backgrounds of blacks."

As December 1979 was coming to a close Locke wrote that he found that many of the people he talked to about the Trait conviction "sharply criticized the jury for the guilty verdict" and were critical of the district attorney's office policy of allegedly preventing a large number of blacks from serving on as jurors in a case where a suspect like Trait had seeming mental problems.

Many told Locke, he wrote, that the pool of prospective jurors should be revised to ensure that a person would not be excluded from a jury because of race, citing Trait's lawyer, Carl Vizzi's complaint about how prosecutors had used their free peremptory challenges to eliminate 13 of the 14 blacks who were in the juror pool in that case.

Locke said many told him they felt the trial judge should be empowered to eliminate from the pool of prospective jurors anyone who is not a member of the same peer group as the defendant.

Locke said he was told by local officials of the National Association for the Advancement of Colored People they were disturbed to find that the background of virtually all the members of the Trait jury "were in no way similar to that of Mrs. Trait."

Locke also cited attorney Vizzi's complaint that prosecutors succeed in getting a "mostly blue-collar" set of jurors for the Trait trial, eliminating the possibility of many white-collar workers who would likely have been more understanding of a mental-illness based defense.

Locke wrote that one local black civil rights activist told him that had Trait been tried by a jury of her peer group it was more likely she would have been found innocent by reason of insanity because "it was obvious to most people that she had to be criminally insane to kill her own children."

Yet despite the large amount of public criticism of the Trait jury verdict, Locke wrote in January 1980 before her sentencing, the comments of a top local mental health official's view that mentally-ill criminals invariably receive better mental health treatment in prison than at a mental institution where they could end of spending the rest of their lives without any chance of a cure.

Dr. Joseph W. Liebergall, assistant director of the Erie County, NY, government's Forensic Mental Health Unit, told Locke that services for treating the criminally insane in mental institutions are generally inferior to the levels of care such an inmate would receive behind bars.

And while a mentally-ill criminal found innocent by reason of insanity and sent by a judge to a mental institution could spend the rest of his or her life there, the penalty health staff at such institutions could determine quickly that the person is no longer a danger to him or herself or to the community and quickly release them with the permission of a judge.

The problem, Liebergall told Locke, was that under New York State criminal law and procedure a criminal found innocent by reason of insanity is not legally required to be fully cured before being released back into the general community.

Liebergall told Locke that the law did not require New York State mental institutions to consider the behavior patterns that may had led a mentally- disturbed criminal to commit a crime in dealing with that patient.

In the prison setting, Liebergall said, prison medical officials working with state parole officials would look into the prior behavior of a mentally-troubled prisoner, his or her behavior at the time of the criminal offense, and currently before releasing them back into general society.

CHAPTER ELEVEN

The Sentencing

With Trait's sentencing set to take place on days later, the $80 million in civil suits filed by her family for the "wrongful" deaths of her four young children were thrown out of court.

On Jan. 21, 1980 State Supreme Court Justice James L. Kane, at the request of Assistant County Attorney Edward J. McGuiness, dismissed the suit against the Erie County government and several county social workers for failing to state a cause of action.

That same day the $40 million suit Trait's mother, Dorothy Williams, filed against the New York State government and the State Social Services Department over the deaths of her grandchildren was removed from the trial calendar of state's Court of Claims on procedural grounds, essentially killing that case also.

But on Jan. 25 as Justice Mintz was prepared to impose sentence on Trait that proceeding was put off for three weeks.

The sentencing was delayed after defense attorney Vizzi told the judge he could provide evidence that one of the male jurors made a racist remark about his client on Dec. 8 in a downtown Buffalo restaurant heard by about a half dozen persons. Vizzi contented that the unnamed white juror had falsely claimed in court he could objectively assess all the evidence and reach a fair verdict.

The judge verbally rebuked Vizzi for having failed to file the proper legal papers outlining the proof of his claims before the scheduled sentencing date, but with no complaint from the prosecution he put off the sentencing to Feb.19.

Before the new sentencing date, the judge ordered Vizzi, to submit to him sworn affidavits of the "five or six" persons who allegedly overheard the juror's allegedly racist comments on Dec. 8.

Vizzi told the judge he had only recently learned of the juror's alleged racial animosity towards the black defendant.

Vizzi claimed that two of the persons who allegedly overheard the juror's racist comments only informed him over the telephone two weeks ago of what he called that "improper conduct." At that time Vizzi told the judge he had been involved in defendant another client in a New York City case and been unable to follow up on the telephoned information. He promised the judge he would file written briefs on the situation.

Also on Jan. 25, Vizzi complained about how Mintz had allegedly allowed the prosecutor Quinlan to make allegedly prejudicial remarks before the jurors.

Vizzi also renewed his complaint about the judge allowing only one black to serve on the jury after prosecutors had voted to excluded at least 13 other prospective black jurors.

Outside the courtroom Vizzi told the news media that the allegedly racially derogatory remark about Trait had been made by one of the white jurors in a downtown restaurant before the trial began.

Vizzi said of that juror: "He said the woman should be locked away, the key should be thrown away. This affects the fundamental right of my client to a fair trial and will result in the overturning of the verdict."

Vizzi, refusing to identify the allegedly racist Buffalo juror, also said he would be renewing his motion to have a new trial in the case take place in New York City.

In Justice Mintz's crowded courtroom on Jan. 25 were a number of persons who identified themselves as members of the Gail Trait Defense Committee.

Outside the courtroom Morris Aiken, who identified himself as chairman of that defense group, said the committee had already raised $1,500 for the Trait defense effort and would keep pressing to see that she is sent to a state mental institution rather than prison.

Aiken claimed the "committee" had "approximately 15" active members who were civil rights activists from the National Association for the Advancement of Colored People, the BUILD civil rights organization of Buffalo, Operation Push, the Community Action Organization and the Urban League.

On Feb. 19, 1980 the sentencing was put off again until Feb. 25 because Vizzi was then representing a client in a trial in Westchester County across the state.

Court observers noted on Feb. 19 that while Vizzi had promised the judge that by Feb. 11 he would have affidavits from six witnesses who allegedly heard one of the trial jurors make what he called a "racist" remark about Trait in a downtown restaurant during the jury trial he never produced such documents.

Trait had been brought to the court house for the scheduled Feb. 19 sentencing, but had to be taken back to the county lockup across the street on Delaware Avenue.

When she was brought back to court on Feb. 25 Justice Mintz imposed the expected maximum prison term of 25 years to life for each of the four murders but made the four life terms concurrent, meaning she would serve a 25 year to life term.

The minimum she faced on the convictions had been a 15 year to life sentence.

Trait's mother, Dorothy Williams, was in the courtroom for the sentencing and burst into tears when the life sentence was imposed.

During the sentencing proceeding the judge spent a majority of the time sharply criticizing Vizzi's handling of the defense case.

While the now-heavy-set Trait remained silent throughout the sentencing proceedings the judge said to Vizzi: "A serious question exists as to whether Gail Trait received proper representation by you in this case." The judge pointedly told Vizzi the appellate court in Rochester should actively consider "your conduct of the defense in this case."

'You alienated jurors to such an extent that may have had an adverse effect on the verdict," the judge told Vizzi. The judge also rebuked Vizzi for his alleged inadequate trial preparation and his failure to make a number of pretrial legal motions. He also faulted the defense attorney for his alleged inability to properly frame questions and his objections to prosecution questioning of witnesses, all of which, the judge insisted, had put off the jurors.

Mintz told Vizzi he felt the defense attorney had alienated the jurors even before evidence was presented at the trial. The judge also noted that even though Vizzi had initially told the jury Trait had committed the killings he had spent the entire trial asking a series of questions of witnesses which the judge said he felt had been "mostly to no avail."

The judge also accused Vizzi of continually violating the gag orders he had placed on him at the start of the trial, saying the defense attorney's constant comments to the news media during the trial caused "much of the publicity this case received."

The judge denied Vizzi's motion to set aside the jury verdict and to order a new trial, prompting the defense attorney to say he planned a vigorous appeal of what he called the jury's "absurd" finding that Trait was legally responsible for her actions.

"In my view, there are far more serious errors by you that deserve and require appellate review," the judge told Vizzi.

"As the trial proceeded you cross-examined and re- cross-examined witnessed for the most part for no purpose," the judge said to Vizzi.

Noting Vizzi's frequent comments to the news media outside the courtroom during the trial the judge told Vizzi he found his "general decorum inexcusable and at times reprehensible."

The judge faulted Vizzi for his apparent lack of preparation of the defense psychiatrists, which he said left them vulnerable on the stand to damaging cross- examination from the prosecutor.

The judge also accused Vizzi of not knowing how to properly ask a question of witnesses and delivering what the judge called a disjointed closing argument to the jury.

The judge said he found the "most damaging testimony" in the trial was that of a jail matron who spoke of how Trait had replayed the killings at the jail.

"You told the jury (that) testimony should be overlooked as a matter of law," Mintz said to Vizzi.

"All these things may have contributed to the unfortunate result of the verdict," Mintz added.

Vizzi, who had frequently clashed with the judge during the four-week trial, agreed that his defense efforts could possibly be one of the appeal issues, noting that he had already arranged to have another attorney argue the actual appeal for him.

But Vizzi then complained about what he called the judge's "outrageous" remarks about him. Stressing that he had what he called a "track record of acquittals" and having lost up to $50,000 in legal fees he otherwise would have earned during the eight weeks he had spent preparing for the Trait trial, Vizzi told the judge he found it "very easy" for the judge "to shift criticism when you should be the subject of criticism."

Vizzi also told Mintz, then a fairly new trial court judge "You were not experienced enough to handle this case, you did not have enough trial experience as a judge. You were not qualified!"

"This verdict was a shock to me and I blame you for the verdict," Vizzi told Mintz.

"How dare you tell me what are the important issues" in the case, Vizzi told Mintz, waiving his finger at the judge and adding "Don't argue with success. I've received many acquittals and would have here but for your conduct. You were for the prosecution. That was very clear. It was like trying a case in front of two prosecutors."

At the end of the judge's estimated 20-minute courtroom criticism of Vizzi he ordered the attorney to file a poor person's appeal for Trait with the Rochester appellate court so the Legal Aid Bureau of Buffalo could be appointed to represent Trait on appeal and include in its appeal the question of whether she had received adequate legal representation. The judge told Vizzi he doubted the Rochester appellate court would allow him to pursue the appeal, having been her court-appointed trial attorney.

The courtroom verbal argument ended with Vizzi accusing the judge of having played to the assembled news media representatives in the courtroom during the trial and judge threatening to hold Vizzi in contempt of court if he continued his complaints.

— News Staff Photographer Richard Roeller

FACES JAIL — A grim Gail Trait walks out of State Supreme Court today after hearing State Supreme Court Justice Joseph D. Mintz sentence her to four concurrent life terms in prison for the July 1978 murders of her three daughters and son. FEB 2 5 1980

A day after the Trait sentencing Michael Beebe, a nationally-known award-winning reporter for the then-Buffalo Evening News, wrote about how some of the Buffalo area's top criminal and civil lawyers had come to the trial to view what he called "the continuing battle between the young Mr. Vizzi and a judge most lawyers consider to be defense-oriented."

Beebe wrote that for "the first time in recent memory here" it seemed "that a lawyer talked back to a Supreme Court justice and got away with it."

Beebe wrote that Mintz' 20-minute lecture to Vizzi during the sentencing "was a law-school primer on how to try a case."

"For most attorneys," Beebe wrote, "it would have been a devastating moment." but "Carl Vizzi waited until it was over and then stood up and gave it right back."

Beebe wrote that "most lawyers and court observers" felt Trait "had a good chance to be acquitted through the insanity defense that Mr. Vizzi used." He also wrote that "Whether Mr. Vizzi alienated and confused the jury, as Justice Mintz suggested, or whether the jury was part of what Mr. Vizzi calls the poisoned atmosphere against the insanity defense in this area, will likely be decided in appeal."

But Beebe also noted in that Feb. 26, 1980 article that Vizzi was "gaining more and more attention for a courtroom style not often seen in Erie County."

A native of the Buffalo northern suburb of Kenmore, the then-31-year-old Vizzi who had graduated from the State University of Buffalo Law School in 1973 and had done his undergraduate work at New York City's Fordham University. He had worked at the New York Legal Aid Bureau from 1973 to 1977 and told Beebe he felt compelled to talk back to judges.

"In the system we have," Vizzi said, "I think it's helpful if you're not on friendly terms with the judge. You have to sac-rifice your client for friendship."

"I just find some of the things that go on in court cases unbelievable and I feel compelled to make comments," Vizzi told Beebe. "I have respect for the (State) Supreme Court," Vizzi said, adding "I don't have respect for all the judges."

Vizzi also categorically denied to Beebe that he had been "headline hunting" during the Trait trial as the judge had accused him.

In the same article Beebe noted that Mintz, had been head of the Buffalo Aid to Indigent Prisoner Society and had played an indirect role in getting Vizzi appointed Trait's court-assigned lawyer. Mints, in 1980 as 46. He had been a lawyer since 1956 and was elected to the bench for the first time in November 1978.

Beebe also noted that a story in The New York Times the prior summer on the conviction of a 15-year- old New York City boy Vizzi had represented in the fatal shooting of a New York fashion designer had noted he had also been repeatedly admonished by the judge in that trial.

Beebe also noted that while the Buffalo Legal Aid Bureau would likely handle the appeal of the Trait murder convictions Vizzi remained active in the Trait case in 1980 because he had been retained by members of a so-called Gail Trait Defense Fund to appeal alleged errors by Justice Mintz during the trial.

Vizzi told Beebe late on Feb. 25, 1980, the day of the sentencing that he was sure "Gail Trait will be out of jail in a year."

CHAPTER TWELVE

Post Sentencing Developments

Hours after the Trait sentencing Buffalo Councilman-at-Large George K. Arthur, a highly respected spokesman for the city's African-American community and a highly-regarded Democratic majority leader of the Buffalo Common Council, the city's legislative body, called for a state investigation of State Supreme Court Justice Mintz.

"The (state) Committee on Judicial Conduct should investigate Justice Mintz because he is not fit or qualified to be a State Supreme Court justice," Arthur told local media representatives.

"If a tragedy of justice has ever been committed it was done when Justice Mintz sentenced Mrs. Trait to four concurrent life jail terms with a minimum on each sentence being 25 years," he added.

"If anyone should go to jail, it should be Justice Mintz," Arthur said. "To deny her proper mental treatment and to sentence her to jail, based on his difference he had with her attorney is a miscarriage of justice."

"It clearly points out that a poor person cannot get a fair trial," Arthur stressed.

Two days after the Trait sentencing Vizzi told this author that on the afternoon of Feb. 26 he had written to Gerald Stern, the administrator of the New York State Judicial Commission, asking him to launch proceedings leading to the removal of Mintz from the bench for what he claimed what that judge's "injudicious and reprehensible" conduct at the murder trial.

Vizzi said that in his letter to Stern he also accused Justice Mintz of having threatened him personally during closed-door proceedings they had during their frequent in-court disputes during the trial.

Vizzi also said that in that letter to Stern he also said he had disclosed that Mintz, before the trial got underway with testimony, had ordered him into his chambers and told him "You (expletive) with me and I'll (expletive) with you." He said he told Stern that he had considered that threat from the judge an effort to get him to "lessen the aggressiveness of my defense."

He said he had, in the letter to the judicial conduct administrator, accused Mintz of improper demeanor on the bench and of frequently making known to the jurors "what his feelings were on the evidence" as it was presented. He said he had also complained of Mintz having "consistently ruled in favor of the prosecution on close issues of law" and about Mintz's alleged errors in his legal instructions to the jury, about his alleged mishandling of numerous legal issues that arose during the four-week trial and the judge's alleged "denigrating" of the defense case before the jurors.

"This was an assigned case" for which he had not been paid despite having spent at least 50 hours preparing witnesses and more time dealing with other pre-trial issues," he said he noted in his letter to Stern.

Justice Mintz, on being informed of Vizzi's letter to Stern, told Buffalo Courier-Express reporter Michael Desmond "I can't make any comment."

Vizzi said he had no objections to the judge's call during the sentencing to have the appeal of the murder conviction handled by the Buffalo Legal Aid Bureau on ineffective assistance of counsel grounds.

"I'm not objecting to someone joining me on the appeal on the grounds of ineffective counsel," Vizzi said. "It's far more likely for a reversal on judicial error and prosecutorial misconduct."

Two days after the sentencing the 50-member Buffalo chapter of the National Bar Association, a predominantly minority-led lawyer's group, said it might file a friend-of-the-court brief on the Trait appeal, according to chapter president James A.W. McLeod.

In confirming that legal group's plans on Feb 28 McLeod, a future Buffalo City Court judge, told News reporter Beebe the group was interested in protecting Ms. Trait's legal rights on appeal.

"We're trying to remove the case from the racial arena and put it in the proper perspective to see her rights are protected in the utmost," McLeod told Beebe.

Three weeks later Vizzi petitioned the Rochester appellate court to grant Trait a "poor person's appeal" and allow him to continue to serve as her co-counsel on the appeal with the Buffalo Legal Aid Bureau. Vizzi also asked the appellate tribunal to reject efforts by the Buffalo chapter of the National Bar Association to intervene, contending that group's announced plans to intervene was a sign of that group's possible "duplicity" with the trial judge and a likely "concoction" designed to deflect appellate criticism of Justice Mintz's handling of the jury trial.

Vizzi on March 18, 1980 told this author that he felt the president of the Buffalo chapter of the National Bar Association, James McLeod, is a personal friend of Justice Mintz "and I believe that the whole maneuver was a concoction that existed between James McLeod and Justice Mintz to deflect criticism away from the judge."

Vizzi also insisted Trait had asked him, in writing, from the Bedford Hills Correctional Facility for women in Westchester County, New York, where she was then serving her sentence, to continue as her attorney.He also insisted that neither Trait nor any members of her family wanted the minority bar group to intervene in the appeal either.

Vizzi also said he saw a potential conflict of interest because some lawyers in the Buffalo chapter of the National Bar Association had represented Trait's estranged husband,

Charles Trait, in civil litigation concerning the deaths of his children.

McLeod told this author that he found Vizzi's claim that his bar group was only interested in protecting the private interests of the judge and its members who had represented Charles Trait "asinine."

McLeod said his organization just wanted to ensure Trait's rights as a minority defendant were protected and because to that he called the "sincere concern" expressed by the organization's membership and by various community leaders about possible mistakes Vizzi made in handling the murder case.

Vizzi declined comment on McLeod's remarks but noted on March 18, 1980 that he had just received a letter from a woman he identified as a "law librarian" at the Bedford Hills prison urging him to get psychiatric treatment for Gail Trait that was not available to her at the prison. Vizzi said the prison worker told him in her letter that she felt it was "obvious" to her that Gail Trait was "in dire need" of psychotherapy.

In Henry D. Locke Jr.'s March 2, 1980 Buffalo Courier-Express column on the Trait case he asked if the criminal justice system was "working against Mrs. Gail Trait."

"Every decision in connection with the case since that unforgettable night (July 16, 19780) when he noted she had "butchered" her four children) has left her holding the losing end of the stick," he wrote.

Locke noted she had been indicted for the murders "even though it was argued that she was mentally ill at the time of the crimes."

"She was ruled capable to stand trial even though defense psychiatrists testified Mrs. Trait was suffering from schizophrenia, paranoid type, and that she did not know the nature or consequences of her actions.

"The prosecuting attorney, George B. Quinlan, probably did not know he had such good friends in

State Supreme Court until he realized most of his motions in the Trait trial were in his favor, and against Carl Vizzi, Mrs. Trait's attorney."

Locke stressed that when he went to court and monitored the proceedings of the four-week jury trial he "observed that many of the times when Vizzi had the floor, State Supreme Court Justice Joseph D. Mintz sat with his hands covering his face.

"But when Quinlan had the floor," Locke went on, "Justice Mintz would most times sit up in his high- backed chair and listen attentively so he could hear every word and observe each move by the prosecutor attorney."

Locke noted that even the selection of the jurors "went against Mrs. Trait."

He noted prosecutor Quinlan "eliminated 13 of the 14 prospective black jurors through his 20 peremptory challenges — a process through which he could remove without having to explain why."

Locke wrote that Adam Jones, the lone black juror on the panel, had admitted "falling asleep during the court proceedings" while claiming that his "sleeping" sessions had really only been "a nod" and claiming that he had not missed any of the trial proceedings.

Locke recalled that Jones had told him that after the Dec. 20 four-count murder verdict that he had been "the last hold-out" on the jury and that he could have caused a so-called hung jury.

Locke also wrote that when Mintz sentenced Mrs. Trait the judge had "indicated he was concerned about the welfare of Mrs. Trait when he criticized Vizzi for allegedly not giving the defendant proper legal representation."

But the judge, in Locke's view, "showed otherwise by sentencing her to a maximum prison term"   even while directing attorneys for the Buffalo Legal Aid Bureau to appeal the jury verdict "on the issue of whether Mrs. Trait was adequately represented during the trial."

In that March 2 column Locke stressed how the area's black civil rights groups and community leaders had "sharply criticized the sentencing," citing George K. Arthur's contention that Justice Mintz should be investigated by the state's Committee on Judicial Conduct and Ellicott Councilman Pitts' description of the Trait life term as "a miscarriage of justice."

Locke wrote that Pitts has issued a statement denouncing the prison term and saying the "tragic case has left a shameful mark on this community and (that) the sensationalism it has generated should be considered embarrassing."

Locke also noted that he had just contacted Pitts, who was then in Richmond, Virginia representing the Buffalo Common Council at the National Conference on a Black America for the 80s.

He said in their telephone call Pitts told him that "in order to correct an apparent miscarriage of justice, a fair, proper and judicious appeal must be made. This can only be done with the assignment of a new attorney with experience and definite concern for justice."

In that column Locke also cited criticism of the Trait conviction that had been publicly issued by Buffalo black civil rights organizations including BUILD (Build, Unity, Independence, Liberty and Dignity), WOMAN (Women on the Move for Action Now) and the Buffalo chapter of the National Association for the Advancement of Colored People.

Pitts called the lengthy prison term Mintz imposed "a miscarriage of justice" and insisted Trait should have been placed in a state mental institution for the treatment he said she needed.

In a legally-binding March 28, 1980 ruling the five- judge Appellate Division of State Supreme Court granted Trait "poor person" status, removed Vizzi from the appeal of the criminal conviction, ordered the Buffalo Legal Aid Bureau to handle her appeal at taxpayer expense and refused to grant "friend-of-court" status in the appeal to the Buffalo chapter of the National Bar Association.

In its brief, the appellate court did not provide a written explanation for its ruling.

Joseph B. Mistrett, then-chief of the Legal Aid Bureau's Appeals Division, told this author of the appellate court's ruling and said: "The way I would interpret the action is that it is now our case exclusively."

Mistrett said he and his legal staff would being work "forthwith" on the Trait appeal.

But a day after the appellate court's ruling Vizzi took issue with claims that he had been removed from the Trait appeal, insisting that it just meant the appellate tribunal was "not appointing me to handle the appeal at taxpayer expense, not that I have been removed from the case."

Claiming that he would be seeking a court order "to keep the Legal Aid Bureau from proceeding on this without me," Vizzi told The Buffalo Courier-Express March 29 "the court doesn't have the right to keep me off the case. They only have the right to determine who will represent her at the public's expense."

Vizzi insisted to the Courier-Express that he had obtained a signed affidavit from Trait expressing her desire that he continue to represent her and claiming no other attorney was "authorized or consented" by her to work on her appeal.

Vizzi told the Courier-Express that a group he identified as the Gail Trait Defense Committee was raising funds to retain him and finance "the very expensive" trial transcript that was "essential" for the appeal.

But that same day James McLeod told The Courier- Express that Vizzi was "out, whether he likes it or not." McLeod also said that with regard to his bar group's offer to get involved as a "friend-of-the-court" on the appeal; "We're out, and he's (Vizzi) out."

Noting the appellate court's decision to grant Trait a "poor person's appeal" of her conviction, McLeod said that as an indigent person she had a right to free appellate counsel "but she doesn't have the right to select who will represent her" at public expense.

On April 27, 1980 the NAACP'S Buffalo chapter passed a resolution agreeing to join with efforts the WOMAN organization in what ultimately proved to be an unsuccessful effort to force the state to move Trait from the Bedford Hills Correctional Facility for women inmates in Westchester County in eastern New York State to a state mental institution while her conviction was being appealed.

Joseph G. Christopher, Buffalo's white so-called 22- caliber killer of black men, was ordered by State Supreme Court Justice William J. Flynn Jr. on Dec. 16, 1981 to undergo pre-trial treatment at a state mental facility for the criminal insane for the slayings of Buffalo area black men a year earlier. That prompted in Black leaders in the Buffalo area to complain to the Associated Press and other news organizations about the apparently racially-unfair treatment Trait had received in the killings of her four young children in 1978 and the life-term she had received in February 1980.

Daniel Acker, then president of the NAACP's Buffalo chapter, told an AP reporter that the Christopher mental treatment ruling was "a miscarriage of justice" in light of the treatment the black Trait had received from the court system.

"She's black. He's white. There's racism going on," Acker said of the Christopher ruling. Asker noted that Justice Flynn ruled prosecutors for the Erie County District Attorney's office had failed to prove "by a preponderance of the evidence" that Christopher in late 1981 understood court proceedings against him and could assist in his own defense.

Masten District Councilman David A. Collins, a black member of the Buffalo Common Council, said Flynn's ruling on the white murder suspect, compared to the treatment the black woman Trait had received, was "a major slap in the face to the black community."

Justice Flynn in his ruling about mental treatment for Christopher, had stressed that it had been an "exceedingly close" legal call because while two prosecution psychiatrists found Christopher to be then mentally competent and fit for trial three defense psychiatrists had ruled he was then mentally incompetent and in need of mental treatment.

Councilman Collins told the AP that "If the same principles were applied to Gail Trait she wouldn't be in jail now." The entire saga of Joseph G. Christopher was outlined by this author in his book "Joey 22" published in 2012.

CHAPTER THIRTEEN

After Ten Years in Prison

O n April 8, 1988 the Rochester, NY-based Appellate
Division of State Supreme Court unanimously overturned Trait's Dec. 19, 1979 jury conviction and
ordered a new trial over the deaths of her four children.

On Feb. 23, 1988 that appellate tribunal heard Buffalo Legal Aid Bureau attorney John A. Ziegler's arguments about
Carl Vizzi's errors both before and during the four-week jury
trial in 1979.

The appellate tribunal, which included Presiding Judge M.
Dolores Denman and Samuel L. Green, both of Buffalo,
agreed with Ziegler that Vizzi had "failed to provide meaningful representation" to Trait.

The decision issued by that appellate tribunal, which cited
"the totality of the omissions, misconduct and errors" Vizzi
made was not credited to any specific appellate judge.

Joining the two Buffalo judges in the case were Justices James H. Boomer and Reuben K. Davis, both of Rochester, and John F. Lawton of Syracuse.

In the new-trial decision the appellate court held that Vizzi's "opening statement was ill-conceived and ineptly developed. It was rambling and disconnected, it elicited 21 sustained objections (from the prosecutor) largely because counsel engaged in argument that was appropriate only for summation (at the end of a trial)." t

Vizzi's "pretrial preparation," the new-trial ruling went on: "was inadequate. His decision to forebear making pretrial motions, in the circumstances of this case, was unwise. He did not appear in opposition to the people's motion for an order precluding pre-trial motions."

And Vizzi's "trial preparation was inadequate to the extent that his direct and cross-examination of witnesses was rendered largely ineffective," the appellate court held.

The appellate panel also faulted what it called Vizzi's often "excessive and purposeless" questioning of prosecution witnesses including his questioning of veteran homicide detectives involved in the investigation.

Noting Vizzi asked the homicide veterans if they had ever been involved in "a more gruesome crime," the appellate panel concluded that further damaged the defense.

Vizzi's "lack of preparation," the appellate court held, "was particularly evident in the examination of defense psychiatrists and thus provided minimal support for the insanity defense. This omission left these witnesses unnecessarily vulnerable to skillful cross-examination which proper preparation could have avoided. The trial court (Mintz) observed that counsel alienated the jurors to such an extent that it may have had an adverse effect on their verdict."

Vizzi's "decorum and deportment," the Rochester judges stressed, "characterized by the court at times as inexcusable and reprehensible, may have contributed to this alienation. Counsel engaged in excessive and purposeless cross-examination of prosecution witnesses. The effect of the answers elicited during this aimless cross-examination of experienced police officers, especially as to whether they had ever witnessed a more gruesome crime, was undoubtedly damaging to the defense."

The Rochester judges also noted Vizzi "declined to cross-examine a jail matron who gave testimony extremely unfavorable to the defense, instead, he simply told the jury on summation to dismiss this testimony as fabricated and incredible."

'We perceive no benefit in further enumerating the numerous examples of errors and misconduct on the part of defense counsel as reflected in this record," the appellate tribunal held. "They were pervasive."

"In sum," the court ruled, 'The totality of the omissions, misconduct and the errors forces the conclusion that counsel's performance deprived defendant of her right to effective assistance of counsel as commanded by the Sixth Amendment of the U.S. Constitution."

In ordering a new trial on the ineffective counsel issues, the Rochester court also refused to rule on appeals attorney Ziegler's complaint about the alleged prejudice of the Erie

County District Attorney's Office which Ziegler had argued was shown by the prosecutor's successful and allegedly improper efforts to ensure that the trial jury had only one black member.

After the Rochester court's ruling John J. DeFranks, Deputy Erie County District Attorney, said the prosecutor's office would be examining that ruling.

But as was customary with such unanimous rulings made by one of the state's intermediate appellate courts, the New York State Court of Appeals, the state's high court, on June 15 refused to consider the Trait case, which meant it was returned to Buffalo for pre- trial preparations.

Until the April 8, 1988 ruling the Trait case had been Erie County's oldest criminal case that had not yet been argued. At that time, many court observers noted, most Western New York criminal cases in the state at that time were argued within about two years of a conviction.

On June 5, 1989 Vizzi, by then a public defender working in Miami, Florida, told this author he felt his "pivotal mistake" in the Trait case had been to expect a jury would or could accept her insanity defense in the mutilation murders of her young son and her three daughters.

"I did the best I could," Vizzi, then 40, told this author, then a Buffalo News reporter. He conceded that he had probably been too young to handle such a complex case and that his own inexperience in such a high-voltage criminal proceeding, the lack of court- provided resources he had been accorded, the assumed prejudice against the insane involved in such actions and what he called the "personality clash" he had with Justice Mintz in the case all contributed to the multiple murder conviction.

Contacted at his office at the Dade County Public Defender's Office in Miami where the native of the Buffalo suburb of Kenmore had worked for three years and become a senior attorney, Vizzi said he found it "shocking" that it had taken nearly a decade in the Buffalo area court system before Trait had been granted a second trial in the case.

Vizzi conceded that he should have asked the judge in the case to appoint a second attorney to work with him in the Trait case or that Mintz should have automatically appointed a second attorney to work on such a high voltage case. He said he felt that being a young lawyer involved with his other legal clients and having no law firm partners and his claim that he had access to few professional resources back then had also hampered his effectiveness in defending Trait.

CHAPTER FOURTEEN

"I Did It"

Brought back to a Buffalo courtroom again on Oct. 12, 1988, the then-35-year-old Trait who had received extensive psychiatric treatment in prison to deal with her diagnosed schizophrenia angrily — and commenting about her children's killings, literally for the first time in public — complained to State Supreme Court Justice Theodore S. Kasler, the supervising justice of all Western New York criminal courts, about what she called the "terrible situation" of being forced to stand trial a second time.

She also took issue with being forced during a second trial to once again face the prospect of having to watch her videotaped confession to police about the killings of her children.

"I (cq) rather plead guilty and go back to Bedford (the women's prison where she had been incarcerated), because I'm not going through this two and three and four times, all this stuff. No! Un-uh! You all (are) not going to put me through this again!," Trait told Kasler,

"I did it," Trait loudly told Kasler in his downtown Buffalo courtroom. "So why do they keep playing that same thing
over and over again? They know I did it. I don't know why
they torture me like this. I cut my wrist before. I'll do it
again. I don't care!"

'I don't want to be listening to that stuff," she loudly continued. "It was a lot of blood and all that stuff like that...I
don't want to go through all that again."

Kasler, saying that he felt the criminal justice system
seemed to be "forcing this woman into total insanity," abruptly concluded that Oct. 12 court session. And he ordered further psychiatric testing of the defendant after Trait said to him
"Let the dead rest in peace." During that court session Trail
also demanded to be sent to the Marcy Correctional Facility,
the New York State prison for the criminally insane where
she had been sent four times for psychiatric treatment while
she had been serving her prison term at the Bedford Hills facility.

After that session court sources told this author that Trait,
after being brought back to Buffalo, had told a psychiatrist
who met with her that she didn't understand why her conviction had been appealed, telling that mental health expert that
"no one asked me" if she had even wanted to appeal.

Also after that Oct. 12 court session, Philip M. Marshall,
the veteran defense attorney and himself a future local judge,
who Kasler had appointed to represent Trait after the April
appellate court ruling, declined to comment on her courtroom
outbursts.

But Marshall said he was confident that if the case proceeds to trial again and Trait is not sent back got the prison for the criminally insane for more treatment that either the charges against her will be quashed on legal grounds he planned to raise or she will be acquitted on insanity issues.

During an Oct. 24 court session Dr. Victoria Besseghini and Dr. Brian Joseph, who Kasler had ordered to conduct psychiatric examinations of Trait, both said they had found her clear-headed enough to understand courtroom proceedings. But Dr. Besseghini stressed to the judge that she found Trait to be mentally ill.

During that court session Trait was allowed to leave the courtroom after telling the judge she found the prospect of reliving the killings of her children "too terrible" to consider.

Commenting on the prospect of again waiting in court for the replaying of her 1978 videotaped murder confession Trait told Kasler "I don't want to hear it.

Please, I don't want to be present. It's too terrible!"

After the judge gave Trait permission to be taken back across the street through an underground tunnel to the Erie County Holding Center where she was held under a suicide watch while awaiting the second trial Trait turned in the courtroom to Erie County Sheriff Deputy Donna Stack who had been assigned to bring her to court and said "Come on Donna, let's get out of here."

As the judge viewed the taped murder confession after Trait was taken from the courtroom Marshall argued that police had improperly obtained the confession from the then-mentally deranged suspect.

In the written report Dr. Besseghini had submitted to the judge that afternoon and which the judge then read into the court record the psychiatrist reported that she found Trait's offer to plead guilty was part of the defendant's desire to return to what Trait felt to be the "comfort and security" of state prison so she would not have to "confront" the nature of her criminal acts against her own children.

The Besseghini written report also indicated she had found in her examination of Trait that being forced to listen once again to her videotaped confession would be "too upsetting" to the defendant.

On Oct. 26 Kasler, without Trait being brought back to court told prosecutors and Marshall that he felt it was too early in the higher-court-ordered proceedings to press Trait further on a possible pre-trial plea.

Noting Trait's recent courtroom outbursts Justice Kasler said he wanted to be sure she was "calm" before discussing a possible plea with her again.

"I want to give her all the time in the world to make that determination," the judge told the attorneys.

Stressing how Trait "became emotional distraught" in her most recent court appearances the judge said he did not want "to give the appearance of coercion" and of improperly pressing the mentally distraught defendant on the issue of a possible guilty plea.

Told on March 28, 1989 that Trait for the past five months had periodically been demanding of her jailers at the Holding Center that she wanted to be sent back to state prison Kasler ordered her brought to court March 31 for a hearing and legal arguments on that issue.

When Trait was brought to Kasler's courtroom on March 31 she repeated her demand to be returned to prison, telling the judge there was no question that she killed her children, butte insisted she could not say whether she had intentionally killed them.

She insisted to the judge that she could not recall her motives for the killings and was afraid of not telling the truth in court.

"I can't lie," Trait told the judge. "God will strike me dead. But everyone knows I did it."

Trait, who had written a letter to Kasler the previous week begging to be returned to prison, told the judge during that March 31 session that she would rather to back to prison then be found insane and sent to a mental hospital.

In prison, Trait told the judge she had been able to do meaningful physical work, got educational training and had become friendly with many of the prison staff.

"In the hospital," she continued, "all they do is give you medication and make you watch TV all day.

There's nothing to do in a hospital. I'd rather do back got prison."

Kasler told Trait he felt her new court-assigned lawyer, Philip M. Marshall, had developed a "strong" insanity defense of her.

Prosecutor Diane M. LaVallee stressed to the judge that the state's higher courts had permitted defendants to plead guilty without admitting criminal intent.

"She doesn't have to actually say she intentionally killed her children," LaVallee told the judge.

Contending that Kasler's ruling a day earlier that prosecutors could use as evidence at a new trial Trait's videotaped murder confession "makes the likelihood of conviction all the greater," LaVallee said. That justified a pre-trial murder plea, the prosecutor added.

With that Kasler told Trait she had to come up with what he told her was valid legal "terminology" by April 7 for him to allow her to make a legally valid guilty plea or he would schedule a murder trial.

Marshall told the judge during that hearing that he had yet to get Trait to say she had deliberately killed her children.

The veteran attorney contended he had developed what he called an "extremely strong, viable defense" of insanity and could prove at trial that Trait had been undergoing "severe" mental problems at the time of the slayings.

On April 7 Trait was brought back to court. She told the judge she had changed her mind and she wanted to stand trial again, using the insanity defense that Marshall convinced her he could use at a non-jury trial.

"I agree with him and I want to take it to trial," Trait said, insisting on a non-jury trial.

When Kasler then told her she would have to formally waive her right to a jury trial she responded, "All right."

Marshall told the judge that the previous week Trait had the wrong impression of the type of treatment she could receive during an expected long-term stay at a state mental hospital should she be found not responsible by reason of insanity.

Since her conviction a decade ago Trait had three times been sent to a state hospital for the criminally insane that lacked both the vocational and rehabilitation programs she had been involved in a the Bedford Hills Correctional Facility for women.

She mistakenly thought she would be denied those types of programs if she was ordered to one of the state's standard mental institutions dealing with non- criminal sufferers, Marshall told Kasler.

During that April 7 court session Prosecutor Diane M. LaVallee told the judge the district attorney's office was "ready for trial." She also unsuccessfully urged the judge to let Trait plead guilty before trial without having to admit intentionally harming her children.

LaVallee insisted that Trait's now-withdrawn demand to be allowed to plead guilty and be sent back to Bedford Hills had been an "intelligent decision." The prosecutor stressed that Trait had realized that should she be sent back to prison she was likely to be paroled in about 15 years, while if sent to a state mental facility for treatment she could end up in such a facility for the rest of her life.

With that Kasler said the non-jury trial would begin before him on May 8.

CHAPTER FIFTEEN

The Second Trial

When the second trial actually got underway on May 16, 1989 George B. Quinlan, then chief of the District Attorney's Supreme Court Bureau, argued that Trait "knew what she was doing" and was not insane when she killed her children during what he called some kind of ritual back in 1978.

Contending prosecutors will be able to prove Trait was not insane at the time of her crimes, Quinlan added, "She knew what she was doing on that very unhappy night." And the prosecutor cautioned Kasler not to make what he called the "pedantic error" of acquitting Trait simply "based on the ghastly nature of the crimes.

Without disclosing their identities, Quinlan also argued that prosecutors would be able to put witnesses on the stand who would be able to describe a plausible motive for her criminal behavior.

Telling the judge he had to "look beyond the hideousness" of Trait's conduct, Quinlan insisted the non-jury trial had to center on "whether or not she should be held accountable for her actions."

Defense attorney Marshall countered by telling the judge he was planning to call to the witness stand six "highly regarded and well-respected medical experts" to establish that Trait was criminally insane when she murdered her children.

The psychiatrists to be called to the stand for the defense should be able to convince the judge that Trait "lacked the substantial capacity" to mentally and intellectually understand what she was doing when she killed her four children "or that her conduct was wrong," Marshall added.

Trait was "not criminally responsible" for the murders and prosecutors will be unable to prove she was not insane that night, Marshall told the judge.

On May 17 retired Buffalo Homicide Chief Leo J. Donovan testified that when he interrogated Trait in the Homicide Squad room at Buffalo Police headquarters hours after the slayings he became convinced Trait "knew what she was doing," even though her conduct that night had been "rather weird."

As he was cross-examined by Marshall the retired homicide chief stressed that he was not a trained psychiatrist and he conceded Trait's actions in the fatal attacks on her own children had not seemed "coherent and logical."

But Donovan told the judge he had come to the conclusion during that video-taped interrogation session that Trait was sincere in her beliefs as she expressed them to him, "that she spoke the truth."

Donovan said he felt Trait had been honestly talking about "what she believed" when she told him and Detective John Ludtka during that interrogation that she felt her children didn't really become her children until she had begun attacking them.

She insisted that it wasn't until she stabbed them and forced them to "confess" to being her children that she felt that night that they actually were her children and that she had carried out those acts to save their souls, Donovan testified.

After nearly a week of prosecution testimony from police and medical examiners and a replaying of Trait's videotaped "confession" hours after the murders attorney Marshall began the defense case, calling to the stand psychiatrists John M. Wadsworth and Brian S. Joseph.

Dr. Wadsworth on May 23, 1989 testified that he found the videotaped "confession" Trait made to police only hours after the murders of her children showing her to be "bizarrely calm" in talking about the killings.

"She said that the children were not hers, which is obviously a delusion," Wadsworth testified about Trait's initial denial to police detectives of being the mother of the victims.

Wadsworth, who examined Trait in the summer of 1978 and again in February 1979 and Dr. Joseph, who was currently treating Trait, both rejected the prosecution case. They both told the judge they had independently found Trait to be suffering from paranoid schizophrenia which they contended sparked the slayings.

"She was deluded when she killed her children and couldn't help it," Dr. Joseph testified.

Dr. Wadsworth, in stressing his rejection of prosecution contentions that the videotaped "confession" showed Trait to be rational and accountable for her actions, insisted her police interrogators had made no effort to question her in what he called the "great depth" needed to assess her state of mind.

During that police interrogation Trait "seemed to be basically aware of what was going on around her, but such psychotics usually have a partial grasp of reality, Wadsworth testified.

Dr. Joseph, who had begun treating Trait in April 1988, told the judge Trait was "certainly subdued" during the police session hours after the killings.

Even currently, in May 1989, Joseph testified, she sometimes becomes confused and incoherent when talking.

"I don't think there's any question that she's schizophrenic," Joseph testified.

Called back to the witness stand on May 31 by prosecutors, Dr. Syed Farooq, one of the two prosecution psychiatrists who insisted at the first trial Trait knew what she had done to her children, repeated his diagnosis.

Farooq told Justice Kasler that Trait had deliberately killed her children because they were "cramping" her allegedly promiscuous "lifestyle."

Farooq testified that he rejected what he called the "rubber-stamp" opinions of other psychiatrist who found Trait to be insane.

He said his own talks with Trait a decade earlier and his review of police records in the case proved to him that she was a troublesome person who quarreled with relatives and frequently did things out of what he called "spite."

"She was not psychotic at that time," Farooq testified about the killings. He said Trait killed her children only ten days after they were returned to her from foster care because "she wanted them out of her hair."

After a day on which she had punished them and force them to eat cold hot dogs Trait grabbed one of her kitchen knives "as a more effective weapon" to use against them after she had beaten them with a shoe, Farooq testified.

Farooq told Kasler he found Trait to have an anti- social personality disorder that makes her hard to deal with, but he insisted she knew she had killed her children and remains criminally accountable for her actions.

Farooq told Kasler the night of the killings Trait had been angry with her mother for refusing to baby-sit her children so she could go out and "party." He said she had a history of sexual promiscuity and drug and alcohol abuse dating back to her teenaged years.

The prosecution psychiatrist insisted Trait's decision to use a knife against her children after she had beaten them with a shoe was a "goal-directed" decision and a clear sign that she knew what she was doing,

Farooq insisted that psychiatrists who claimed Trait was insane only did so in an effort to remain consistent with the findings of colleagues.

"All these people (other psychiatrists) started singing a chorus" in mutually agreeing, incorrectly, that Trait was insane, Farooq told Justice Kasler.

On June 1, 1989 prosecutors gave defense attorney Marshall the Erie County Medical Center records on Trait's treatment there right after the fatal attack.

The defense attorney noted the hospital records showed that allegedly incriminating remarks Trait had made to one of her female guards in the hospital's prisoner-lockup ward four days after the killings had come after she had to be handcuffed and sedated.

The hospital records showed she had been handcuffed and sedated at the time because she had become angry and unruly after a hospital psychiatrist told her why she had been hospitalized.

Called to the stand at the non-jury trial Erie County Sheriff's Deputy Marcia B. Kruzynski, a key prosecution witness at the 1979 jury trial, testified that as Trait talked to her in a guarded room at the hospital on July 21, 1978 — after she was handcuffed and sedated — she said "I know, now, what I did." And then, Kruzynski told the judge, Trait calmly described the butcher-knife murders.

Defense attorney Marshall showed the judge that the transcripts of the 1979 jury trial showed Kruzynski testifying under questioning only from prosecutors that Trait had told her during that hospital session that "she knew exactly what she was doing" during the   killings.

Marshall told the judge that Kruzynski's latest testimony showed decisively that she had not been properly cross-examined and forced to clarify to the jury at the 1979 trial the details of that allegedly incriminating July 1978 statement by Trait.

Marshall contended the deputy's new testimony clearly showed Trait had not been aware of what she had done in the summer of 1978.

Kruzynski, a former hospital nurse's aide, testified in response to Marshall's questions, that Trait in the hospital in July 1978 had sounded "rational" as she talked about the children's murders, but she said Trait also wondered to her at that time "if she was going to get the electric chair for what she had done."

Kruzynski also conceded under Marshall's questioning that hospital records showed a psychiatrists had warned hospital workers in July 1978 not to talk to Trait. She said on July 21, 1978 Trait had asked her for a cigarette and did all the talking herself.

Kruzynski told the judge that when she had been a hospital nurse's aide she had dealt extensively with mentally disturbed patients. She acknowledged under questioning from defense attorney Marshall that at the hospital and later at the Erie County Holding Center, she observed Trait suffering psychotic episodes in the women's cellblock where she had been regularly stationed as a guard.

In closing arguments on June 1, 1989 Prosecutor George B. Quinlan denounced the defense psychiatrists as what he called "courtroom charlatans" who had offered what he told the judge had been a "psychiatric smorgasbord" of insanity claims. The prosecutor insisted the defense psychiatrists had failed to review the "how and why" of how an alleged psychosis could have sparked the mutilation murders.

Urging Kasler not to be "hoodwinked" by the defense psychiatric claims, the prosecutor said all the evidence showed Trait had been known for a long time by her family and friends for having what he called a "deeply abiding spitefulness" that prompted her homicidal actions against her own children.

Like the prosecutor, defense attorney Philip M. Marshall cited Trait's 30-minute video-taped "confession" to police hours after the murders in his closing argument.

Marshall described Trait as a "grievously-ill woman guided by a mind that had been short-circuited" by the paranoid schizophrenia that a dozen psychiatrists and psychologists had diagnosed through the years.

Kasler told the attorneys to return to court at 9:30 a.m. Monday, June 5 for his verdict. He said he wanted to review evidence before issuing the decision that will either send Trait back to prison or to a state mental hospital.

On June 5 Kasler ruled that he found Trait legally insane in carrying out the mutilation murders of her four children 11 years ago.

Setting the stage for possibly years of mental hospital treatment for the then-35-year-old woman, Kasler held that she was not criminally responsible for either the intentional or depraved murders of her young ones.

Kasler, not publicly disclosing the evidence that brought him to his verdict, cited the state's criminal insanity law in finding Trait not responsible by reason of mental illness or defect on the eight counts of murder that had been lodged against her.

Has the judge found Trait guilty of any of the murder counts she would still have been eligible for parole consideration in about 15 years.

State law at that time did not set a maximum amount of time she would have to be kept in mental confinement on the not-responsible verdict, but provided that it would be up to a judge to consider and possibly approve any change in her status during her mental hospitalization, including the possibility that she could be allowed limited off-grounds release times at whatever mental institution she was being treated.

Kasler, after a three-week bench or non-jury trial in the case, declined further comment on the case either on the bench or later.

Speaking for the first time since the start of her second trial, Trait, right after Kasler rendered his verdict looked up at the judge and said: "Thank you, your honor."

Having been stabilized mentally in recent years in p through the application of strong anti-psychotic medication in prison, as Trait was being taken from the courtroom she said to news media representatives "I don't want to be in society. I'm happy because I'm going to stay the rest of my life" in mental institutions.

As Phillip M. Marshall, her latest and successful defense attorney, left court he said he felt that with proper psychiatric care in the state's mental institutions he believed Trait could get hospital-leave privileges within several years.

Because of the not-guilty by reason of insanity verdict Trait, under state law, had to be examined within the next 30 days by two psychiatrists to determine whether her initial mental hospital stay would be in a guarded ward if she was determined to still be a danger to herself or be place in just a general ward.

Marshall that morning said he found fault with the way Carl Vizzi had handled Trait's defense years earlier. Marshall stressed that he presented Kasler with the findings of 12 psychiatrists who examined Trait to "undo the poor work that my predecessor did" on the case.

"I don't think she should have been convicted in the first place," Marshall said. He contended Trait's conviction really stemmed from community revulsion at the nature of the killings.

Marshall said he was sure Trait's mental illness remained "treatable" and controllable. He said he was confident in predicting she will not be spending the rest of her life in mental confinement.

Marshall said he was sure Trait's long-standing paranoid schizophrenia was "treatable" with new drugs and therapies then emerging.

"I'm not a psychiatrist," Marshall said, "but I think the day will come when she is set free."

Later that morning then-Erie County District Attorney Kevin M. Dillon conceded that his prosecution team assigned to the case had what he described as "a very difficult" time trying to overcome a decade of evidence that had been developed about Trait's mental condition.

Justice Kasler, based on the findings of court-appointed psychiatrists who had examined Trait since the non-jury trial, on Sept. 11, 1989, ordered her to undergo at least the first six months of her mental treatment in a guarded state psychiatric facility.

Kasler opted not to put her in a standard ward of a mental institution because he said recent examinations had led state psychiatrists to consider that even with her noticeable improvements in day-to-day behavior she still remained a potential danger to her own physical safety.

Philip M. Marshall, Trait's latest attorney, told the judge on Sept. 11, 1989 that Trait would not be contesting the most recent psychiatric findings because "she does recognize the need for further treatment."

Kasler, during that court session, said he based his order on reports from psychiatrists at the state's Mid-Hudson Psychiatric Center which indicated that while Trait had been "cooperative" with hospital staffers since the non-jury trial she still suffered periods of depression concerning the loss of her children that left her dangerously suicidal.

Vizzi, contacted in Miami, Florida by this author several hours after the insanity verdict, stressed that he felt he had done "the best that I could" a decade ago.

Vizzi cited his own inexperience over a decade earlier in dealing with such a complex criminal case, community prejudice stemming from the brutality of the killings of such young children and his lack of court-provided resources that could have made his job easier.

By then a public defender in the Florida justice system, Vizzi said he always felt confident Trait would be granted a second trial and found not-responsible criminally.

He said his efforts to successfully present an insanity defense at the first trial to what he called a highly skeptical jury was hindered by what he called the "acrimonious" sentiments he was experiencing from court officials, prosecutors and even some in the news media.

"The tragic part of this is that it took ten years to get a retrial," Vizzi said, citing the backlog of criminal cases that existed in Western New York for such poor-person defendants.

Vizzi called Justice Kasler "courageous" for correctly deciding the criminal case based on all the proper psychiatric evidence of Trait's mental problems.

He also complained that Buffalo-area court officials over a decade earlier had not given him enough time to prepare a proper insanity defense.

Vizzi also spoke of what he called the "wrong chemistry" that had developed between him and Justice Joseph D. Mintz, both before and during the jury trial.

He also criticized the Rochester appellate court for faulting his handling of the case as one of its main reasons for ordering a second trial.

Vizzi said that appellate court failed to address what he called a central issue in the first trial, that being the lack of an adequate pool of prospective black jurors able to hear the case. It was the "systematic exclusion" of blacks from the jury by prosecutors and supported by Mintz's rulings that had denied Trait a fair jury trial, he said.

Vizzi conceded that a decade earlier he had only had about two years of experience being a court- appointed lawyer for such poor defendants as Trait. But he stressed that he had what he felt was "no backing at all" from court officials as he had unsuccessfully sought permission to obtain court funds to hire New York City psychiatrists to examine Trait before the jury trial.

He also expressed what he called his own "frustration and anger" at the Buffalo jury that convicted Trait. But Vizzi conceded that his decision to press ahead with a jury trial had been "a strategic error on my part" because of what he called the systematic "reluctance" of trial juries to acquit defendants on insanity grounds.

He said he knew the jury trial situation as it had been developing was "destined to be a disastrous "undertaking.

"I wish I would have had help," the by-then- seasoned attorney lamented.

Sadly, Vizzi, died in Miami Beach, Florida on Jan.27, 1993 at the age of only 45 from complications linked to pneumonia he had been suffering from for several months. Vizzi by then had worked as a public defender for Dade County for 12 years, according to his sister, Belle Lancaster

With Trait then 39 and in treatment in a New York State mental institution, Vizzi was survived by his wife, Jacqueline, two sons and a daughter. A Mass was said for him the day of his death in St. Patrick's Catholic Church in Miami Beach.

CHAPTER SIXTEEN

Buffalo's Guardian Angel

Trait's case prompted Constance Boyle Eve, a much-respected Buffalo-area educator and community activist, to launch in a Buffalo storefront what she called The Women For Human Rights and Dignity organization to provide an alternative living site for women suffering domestic abuse or possible prison- time for minor crime.

Mrs. Eve was the wife of Arthur O. Eve., then-deputy speaker of the New York State Assembly and the most powerful African-American political figure in Western New York.

A well-known and acclaimed local educator and mother of five who held a master's degree, Mrs. Eve had been active for years in Buffalo area religious, professional, political, civic and service organizations.

She had gone to see the just-jailed Trait while she was under a suicide watch at the Erie County Holding Center in 1978.

In late October 1989 Mrs. Eve told Louise Continelli, a Buffalo News staff reporter, that with the organization she wanted to start she would be "just trying to scratch the surface" of single parent women like Trait who were under increasing pressure to raise families during severe cutbacks in government financial support for them.

Not referring directly to Trait, Mrs. Eve told Continelli that the vast majority of young women who get in trouble with the law were unemployed, "uneducated, and they're unskilled."

Working through the Women for Human Rights and Dignity organization Mrs. Eve opened a Women's Residential Center in Buffalo where women convicted of minor crimes could be sentenced by local judges as an alternative to jails.

Through her organization such troubled young women were encouraged to get their high school degrees and advance educationally and to seek careers such as nurses and word processors while living in a residential facility rather than in jail.

Mrs. Eve also founded Project JOY which annually provided prison workshops for incarcerated women and provided them with Christmas gifts they could send to their children.

By the end of December 1992 Mrs. Eve had Women for Human Rights and Dignity humming, opening three new facilities that year.

On Dec. 19, 1992 she and the Rev. Julius D. Jackson, rector of St. Philip's Episcopal Church, took about 50 persons on a tour of the facilities with her telling everyone:

"There is so much to be done and we have so little time to overcome years of problems," Mrs. Eve said.

The tour that day began at the Women's Residential Resource Center at 2528 Main Street there ten women were then living instead of serving jail sentences. At that center the women, in a family friendly setting, got counseling and treatment.

Mrs. Eve noted that within about a month at Main Street and Florence Avenue her Transitional Home would be opening to house five woman who would, not be sent there as a replacement for a jail term, but because they wanted help and training to become self- sufficient and get their children back from county and state programs.

She noted that at the old Crawford Monument building at 2337 Main Street work was underway then to remodel it into the One Stop Center for Women housing a Center for Educational/Vocational Enrichment programs with classes covering basic skills and completion of courses leading to a high school equivalency diploma, vocational education and hands-on experience in budgeting, nutrition and parenting. That facility would also house a center for ceramic arts, needle work and music, she noted.

The last stop of that tour that day was at the Dignity Circle off Humboldt Parkway on a street previously known as Buell Street.

That facility was the last one that women being helped by the program would be placed before they strike out on their own, Mrs. Eve said.

That facility included eight duplex homes and two single-family homes along with a service building. And prices for those residences were to be kept within the price range of women just getting back into the local job market or entering it for the first time, she said.

Mrs. Eve told the news media that day that she expected the average stay in her program would be about two years.

"That should give our women plenty of time to get their children back and find a job that will get them off welfare and give them the ability to take care of the family," she said. "It will also give them time to adjust to a return to the world outside of our organization."

On the tour with Mrs. Eve that day were three well known and highly respected local judges, including two of the area's top African-American judges, Rose H. Sconiers and Robert T. Russell and then-State Supreme Court Justice Barbara Howe.

Justice Howe later become the Erie County Surrogate Judge and Judge Sconiers became a State Supreme Court Justice and ultimately a justice of the Appellate Division, Fourth Department in Rochester, which overall all courts in the state's western regions.

Buffalo City Court Judge Russell gained international fame by heading that City Court's Drug Court and creating in 2008 the first "veterans' court" in the United States which dealt with issues unique to military veterans, such as Post

Traumatic Stress Disorder caused by combat experience. Because of Russell's efforts is dealing with trouble military veterans in April 2010 he was honored by U.S. Secretary of Veterans Affairs, Eric Shinseki.

During the December 1992 tour with the judges Mrs. Eve recalled that her involvement in the effort to help troubled women had been prompted by her distress over what had happened to Gail Trait.

Arthur O. Eve, Mrs. Eve's husband and said of his wife that day that "God makes everything happen, and from something bad, something good can occur," as his wife was then proving.

Mrs. Eve, the mother of five grown children, on April 25, 1998 at ceremonies in Atlanta, Georgia, was presented the 1998 National Alexis de Tocqueville Award, the most prestigious honor bestowed by the United Way of America.

Before a meeting of more than 2000 volunteers from the United States and Canada who were attending the United Way's Community Leaders Conference, Mrs. Eve was presented the de Tocqueville award.

Others who had been honored with the de Tocqueville Award were former U.S. presidents Jimmy Carter and Ronald Reagan, entertainer Bob Hope, auto magnate Henry Ford II and former National Football League Commissioner Pete Rozelle.

Robert M. Bennett, then president of the United Way of Buffalo and Erie County, who had nominated Mrs. Eve for the national award — which resulted in her becoming the first Western New York recipient of that honor — said of her:

"The de Tocqueville Award is particularly for volunteer leadership, and I am sure there are not many people in Western New York who have recruited the number of volunteers and dealt with the issues that Connie deals with."

When Mrs. Eve, an English professor emeritus at the Erie County Community College in Buffalo, where she formally retired after only 32 years of work, spoke to Agnes Palazzetti, a famed Buffalo News reporter, in April 1998 about the de Tocqueville award she was going to receive she said of Gail Trait:

"I remember thinking...that there was no one there to help this poor, sick mother through her ordeal and if she ever is released from a prison mental hospital would there be anyone waiting to help her back into the outside world?"

She said Trait's plight had prompted her to form Women for Human Rights and Dignity which grew into a multifacility operation with trained staff to intervene before a woman is incarcerated and even if sent to jail provide them with support, education, training and housing to help them achieve independence for themselves and their children.

Under the Project Joy program Mrs. Eve annually took a busload of volunteers at Christmas time to visit women inmates at the Albion Correctional Facility for Woman and the Erie County Correctional Facility in Alden.

Under that program the Eve volunteers took thousands of dollars' worth of donated gifts that the incarcerated women could pick gifts for their children.

In 1988 Michael Morse, then-deputy superintendent of the Albion facility, said of Mrs. Eve's efforts:

"Constance Eve is not only a tremendous individual and tireless volunteer but when she comes to our facility each Christmas season, she brings her scores of volunteers from the Buffalo area as outstanding as herself."

The Project Joy efforts for jailed women unable to spend Christmas with their families, enabled those women to select gifts which were then gift-wrapped and delivered to their children by Mrs. Eve and her volunteers.

Also in April 1988 Gerald Redden, then-business agent for the Plumbers and Steamfitters Labor Local 22 in the Buffalo area, told Palazzetti of Mrs. Eve:

"Every time Connie has called, we are there. You just don't say no to her," Redden said.

Recalling the first time he walked into the first building Mrs. Eve had acquired for her organization, Redden said he found it had a water problem.

"When she saw me, she looked at me like I was an angel who was going to save her," Redden said. "Not only do our people donate their time," Redden said, "But we have had contractors voluntarily donate materials" to support the efforts of Mrs. Eve who also raised thousands of dollars in donations as she acquired buildings, community residences and a duplex complex for her program to help troubled women reach their goal of independence.

People that Palazzetti spoke to about Mrs. Eve that month stressed that Mrs. Eve was never shy about turning on her winning personality to gain expert and free labor to restore and remodel the older buildings her organization had acquired.

Mrs. Eve told Palazzetti that month that "The first year we went to Albion" for the Project Joy effort "there were 58 woman there who were parents, and they were serving time for petty things. Last year when we went, there were 1,460 women. Two-thirds of them were either parents or of child-bearing age. There were young women of 16, angry with the world, and most of the women were there because of crack cocaine."

She also told Palazzetti of her own upbringing as one of a family of 10 children.

"However meager things might have been," she said of her family "we always had hope. That's what we have to do. Give these women and their children hope."

Mrs. Eve told Buffalo News reporter Deidre Williams in December 2007 that the first time she saw Gail Trait in 1978 under a jail suicide watch was an image she would never forget as long as she lived.

"She looked like an animal," Mrs. Eve said of the jailed Trait. "She was disheveled. She was bloated from the medication they were giving her, and her hair looked like twigs growing out of it. She was stripped of her dignity, and that's the most valuable gift you have."

In an article published on Christmas Day 2007 Williams noted that the Women for Human Rights and Dignity organization Mrs. Eve established in 1978 after her visit to Trait in that downtown Buffalo lockup had by the end of that year dealt with "tens of thousands of women" in similar down-trodden situations.

As part of her efforts to help socially-downtrodden women Mrs. Eve in 1980 established Project Joy and with its volunteers which ranged from local judges to gospel singers made an annual Christmas time visit to the women serving time at New York State's Albion Correctional Facility, a medium-security prison that looked like a school except for the razor wire that ringed the facility.

For a Dec. 7, 2003 Buffalo News article on the Project Joy holiday prison visits reporter Sandra Tan spoke to inmates and project volunteers in describing how that effort, which by then involved more than 80 volunteers, gave the incarcerated women what she called "a reason to look forward to living."

Benika Casselman, an Albion inmate from Lockport, New York, told Tan how surprised she had been to see judges who sentenced people to jail giving the inmates words of encouragement during the Project Joy visits.

"A lot of times, you think you're never going to get out of here," Casselman told the reporter. "There are these judges here telling you there's hope for you.

You'd think judges would be against you. These people are thinking of us. Sometimes you think when you're in here, nobody thinks of you."

Tan who went to the 2003 Albion holiday celebration staged in the cafeteria hall of that prison, quoted then- Buffalo City Court Judge E. Jeanette Ogden, later a New York State Supreme Court justice, telling the women inmates:

"One day you are going to leave this facility. You always have to believe one day you're going to leave. We're here to tell you there is some relief. When you have paid your debt to society, you have the right to share in the rights of society. Be positive, my sisters, have hope!"

Tan noted that during the 2003 Project Joy event at Albion some 1100 inmates in groups spent several hours each dancing, singing and listening to words from the volunteers in the cafeteria before heading back to their cells carrying gift bags they were given.

Mrs. Eve told Tan for that 2003 article that the goal of the Project Joy prison events was to "lift up" the female inmates and "give them hope" because having hope was "half the battle" for them to turn their lives around.

For the December 2007 Buffalo News article Mrs. Eve told Deidre Williams the premise of her organization remained to "empower women, children and families toward economic, emotional and social growth."

During her December 2007 interview Mrs. Eve said that giving women back their dignity was the mission of her organization, including through Project Joy. By

The first Project Joy event at the Albion prison attracted 156 jailed women and as of 2006 some 1,700 incarcerated women took part in the Project Joy events, she noted.

For that article longtime Project Joy volunteer Carolyn Burke, who met Mrs. Eve while serving a drug selling sentence at Albion until 1996, told Williams she had run away from her home in New York City at the age of 9.

Burke, who said she went back to Albion every year since her 1996 release, said she told incarcerated woman "they can't stay struck."

"Just by me being there, I give them inspiration," Burke, who completed her post-prison parole in 2000, told Williams.

"Before, my life was about jail and the streets.

Today, I can say I have my own apartment," Burke said. Burke also said she was also in the process of getting her high school equivalency degree.

Williams wrote about how a component of Mrs. Eve's Project Joy holiday event always involved holiday gifts and food giveaways for families found to be facing difficult times.

And since 1985 Mrs. Eve's Women's Residential Resources Center on Main Street in Buffalo functioned as an alternative to jail for women who had received one-year sentences for misdemeanors and even some felony offenses.

Eddie D. Watson-Keels, director of the Women's Residential Resource Center, told Williams that women were sent to that facility from Buffalo City Court, the Buffalo Drug Court, the Erie County, New York, Department of Probation and the New York State Department of Parole.

The Residential Resource Center had ten beds available for women generally found to be between the ages of 30 to 45. They also had mental health services, substance abuse counseling and high school equivalency and pre-colleges classes available at the Eve organization's Center for Educational/Vocational Enrichment at Main Street and Leroy Avenue, Williams was told.

Tanya Ervin, then working as a counselor at the Buffalo Psychiatric Center while she was continuing to take college classes to get a degree in counseling, told Williams that the program formerly incarcerated woman had to follow under the Eve agencies were "strict, very strict."

Ervin said she learned about that strictness the hard way when she was sent to the program in 1998 and got kicked out. She said she returned to the program in 2001and graduated, getting her job at the state mental facility in Buffalo and continuing to take college courses to eventually get a bachelor's degree.

"My life has changed because of the program," Ervin said. "They are an inspiration. They teach us about living life on life's terms, and if you're not used to that, it seems very hard. They help us understand that in the simplest terms."

The Buffalo News reporter found that once women graduated from the residential center they could move into the Dignity Village near Humboldt Parkway in Buffalo with their children.

That village provided 20 units of affordable duplex housing with on-site services including family activities, help dealing with human service agencies and programs in parenting skills and conflict resolution.

Mrs. Eve told the reporter the whole effort was to "let us keep our dignity. And when we have that, we're rich."

During the silver anniversary celebration of Women for Human Rights and Dignity which attracted over 1,000 persons to the Buffalo Convention Center on April 24, 2004 Mrs. Eve was presented a Superior Volunteer Award for her 25 years of commitment to the organization she had founded and for all the human services it provided.

In accepting the award that afternoon Mrs. Eve humbly spoke of how the plight of Gail Trait had prompted her to start the rights organization.

She told the crowd "Gail was robbed of her dignity. Let us keep our dignity, and when we have that, we're rich."

For the 25th annual holiday gathering of Project Joy with some eleven hundred female inmates assembled in the mess hall of the Albion Correctional Facility on Dec. 4, 2004, Mrs. Eve told Buffalo News reporter Lou Michel that her efforts had been inspired by the fact that she knew most of those inmates "were the heads of single-parent families before their incarceration." Mrs. Eve said she knew of the obstacles the former inmates would be facing and that's what she and the staff were working to help them overcome.

At the Project Joy's Dec. 2, 2006 presentation before more than 1,200 female inmates at the Albion Correctional Facility Mrs. Eve told Buffalo News reporter Louise Continelli her efforts and the efforts of the 70 volunteers who came with her to provide the inmates with gifts for them and their children and loved ones and counseling on a number of themes ranging from legal to medical matters was all designed to give them back their "sense of self-worth."

A week later at Project Joy's holiday celebration for more than 1,000 Buffalo children, parents and caregivers at Buffalo's Dr. Lydia T. Wright School of Excellence on Oppenheimer Street Mrs. Eve told Buffalo News reporter Deidre Williams that effort was part of her organization's efforts to expand the economic, emotional and social growth of all the area's children and families.

The daylong Project Joy Christmas season program ran at the Albion prison for 31 years until it was permanently moved to the Lydia T. Wright School of Excellence in 2009 and reconfigured to focus on parents and guardians.

In 2011 officials at Buffalo's Canisius College agreed to archive the three decades of efforts of Mrs. Eve's Woman for Human Rights and Dignity organization to provide assistance to incarcerated women.

CHAPTER SEVENTEEN

Back in Buffalo

After almost a decade of real mental treatment for her paranoid schizophrenia Gail Trait made her first unsupervised visit back to Buffalo the first week of September 1998.

By then Trait was been living in a group home near the state's Elmira Psychiatric Center where she was being treated. She took a bus for the trip to Buffalo to visit an ailing an elderly aunt. She stayed with her ailing aunt in that woman's apartment in Buffalo's Bailey- Kensington area.

Trait, then 46, told Buffalo News reporter Lou Michel it had been a painful homecoming.

"It feels terrible," she told Michel shortly after that visit to her ailing aunt, who begged not to be publicly identified because of her fears that some members of even her own community would denounce her for her belief in her niece's innocence and recovery from her horrifying mental ailment.

'I have some very bad memories," Trait told Michel. "I have a lot of remorse for what has happened."

Trait said giving her life to God and all the medication and counseling she received over the past decade helped her regain her sanity.

Also speaking to Michel, Trait's aunt told him she had talked to Trait about how her oldest child, her daughter Kylia, had she lived to September 1998 would have been nearing her 30th birthday. The elderly woman insisted the killings of Trait's children were a "one-time thing" and happened "because she just lost it. A mother would have to go off the deep end to kill her own children!"

Trait's cousin, Nafeesah Woods, told Michel that society shared in the blame for the tragedy.

"Gail killed her children, but New York State helped her," Nafeesah said. "The children weren't supposed to be alone with Gail. She needed psychiatric help."

Trait's elderly aunt stressed to the reporter that when the killings were underway Trait "didn't know it happened" because of her mental problems.

"But now she realizes it and has a lot of remorse," the elderly woman said. "She knows it will never go away. She missed her children quite a bit. While Gail was in prison she got saved. She got to know the Lord and it lead her to a closer walk with Him. That helped her."

By 1998 Trait had gone back to using her birth name of Gail Williams.

Her aunt and cousin told Michel they were thrilled by the progress they said she seemed to have made with her health problems.

Trait by 1998 was living in the group home and was working full-time in a Seneca Falls store. From time to time she was even going out on dates and writing poetry. Her relatives said she had no desire to move back to Buffalo after she was formally released from treatment at the Elmira facility.

Michel got a different view of Trait's condition in 1998 from then-Buffalo Police Commissioner Rocco J. Diina and William P. Conwell, then assistant chief of detectives of the Buffalo Police Department.

Diina insisted persons like Trait found innocent of criminal activity by reason of insanity need supervision for a lifetime because of the likelihood that some will eventually become violent once more.

Conwell had been one of the first police officers to go into Trait's second-floor flat and witness the severely mutilated bodies of her four young children, something that in 1998 he still found "horrible and sad" to contemplate.

Conwell insisted that any individual found criminally insane should be forced to remain institutionalized for a lifetime.

"Who's to judge if she (Trait) is sane, psychiatrists who write the rules themselves? I don't think so," Conwell told the reporter, "How about her children? When they can give an answer on that, then she can be released."

The police commissioner confirmed that officials at the Elmira Psychiatric Center had notified Buffalo police in advance of Trait's September 1998 trip to Buffalo.

The commissioner said he felt police should also be formally notified whenever Trait is officially discharged from state mental treatment.

Trait's elder aunt and her cousin, Nafeesah Woods, stressed to Michel that Trait told them she planned to continued receiving professional counseling and taking antipsychotic medications once she was formally released from state mental treatment program.

They both said they believed she could be a good citizen.

Miss Woods noted that Trait the weekend of her 1998 visit had changed the diaper of her 8-month-old son effortlessly.

"The bottom line to all of this," Miss Woods said, "is she's mentally healthy now and she's not a serial killer or someone sadistic!"

Trait's elderly aunt said she could foresee Gail being burdened psychologically for the rest of her life over the deaths of her children. But she felt she would be able to deal with that in a bearable manner.

"The good thing," Trait's elderly aunt said, "is that Gail believes she'll see her children again someday with the Lord if she keeps her faith. She believes that they're in heaven and no harm can come to them." Michel later became a famed and nationally-known police and crime reporter and was recognized by numerous military organizations for his numerous Buffalo News stories about Western New York veterans of military combat.

CHAPTER EIGHTEEN

A Belated Oops!

After the 1979 Trait trial State Supreme Court Justice Mintz went on to a magnificent career on the bench. But as he was being forced to leave the active bench under the state's mandatory age 76 retirement rule for state judges he admitted that her case was his judicial "baptism under fire."

Months before he had to step down from the active bench at the end of 2009 Mintz told Buffalo Business First reporter Matt Chandler that he had been assigned the Trait case because he was a relatively new trial court judge, having taken the bench in January 1979.

He said he was "convinced" before the jury trial that Trait "had serious psychiatric problems, but the DA's office wasn't interested in hearing that." And while he said he "frankly thought the lawyer (Vizzi) made some fundamental errors" he had been reluctant to grant a mistrial because I was afraid of running afoul of double jeopardy"

On Dec. 20, 1979 the State Supreme Court jury before Mintz found Trait guilty and set the stage for her near-decade-long stay in state prison. That jury verdict was overturned on April 8, 1988.

Though Mintz didn't mention it specifically to the Business First reporter the five-judge Rochester appellate tribunal, in ordering another trial, specifically faulted defense attorney Vizzi for having "failed to provide meaningful representation" to Trait.

The appellate court cited what it called Vizzi's "inadequate" pretrial preparation and his "rambling and disconnected" opening statement before the jury and Mintz.

When this author contacted Vizzi In June 1989 he stressed what he called the "acrimonious" nature of the 1979 prosecution case and the "wrong chemistry" that had developed between him and Justice Mintz.

At that time Vizzi lauded State Supreme Court Justice Kasler for what he called that judge's "courageous" decision to rule Trait legally insane.

Vizzi also faulted the Rochester appeals court for failing to address what he said he had always found to have been a central issue at the first trial — the lack of an adequate pools of possible black jurors to hear the case.

Conceding that in 1979 he had only two years of experience as a private defense attorney, Vizzi said he felt what he called the "systematic exclusion" of blacks from the initial jury pool had denied Trait a fair trial. But he also conceded that his decision to go with a jury trial had been "a strategic error on my part because of the longstanding "reluctance" of juries to acquit criminal defendants on insanity grounds.

Vizzi said he had a feeling before the 1979 trial got under way that what lay ahead was "destined to be a disastrous" proceeding.

"The tragic part of this is that it took 10 years to get a re-trial" because of the deep backlog of appeals for poor persons like Trait in the Buffalo area. Vizzi noted during the 1989 interview.

CHAPTER NINETEEN

More Angels

The Slaughter of the Innocents continued.

By the early 21st century the overworked child protection workers in the Erie County Government's Social Services Department which dealt with Buffalo, New York and surrounding communities were dealing, annually, in some years, with over 12,000 complaints of child abuse and neglect.

So much for the political progressives' view about The Great Society and the rapid increase in U.S.

President Lyndon B. Johnson's War on Poverty launched in the 1960s.

Those government efforts ended up destroying many lower class families and lead to rapid increases in unwed child births and rapid increases in the use of illegal drugs and related criminal activities.

By the start of the second decade of the 21st century Erie County had 80 caseworkers certified to handle child abuse cases. They were handling, by 2012, some 12,181 complaints annually.

By that decade things got so bad that Child Protection caseworkers each had to deal simultaneously with up to 50 cases. That situation caused overtime expenses to dramatically increase for the county government and forced department managers to get directly involved in dealing with allegations of child abuse and neglect.

As 2014 began seven caseworkers had resigned, six were terminated for failing probation mandates or other situations, two former caseworkers returned from other jobs in the county government and three other caseworkers were out on medical leaves.

The situation got so bad that 126 child protection caseworker lines were admit to the Erie County government's budget by 2014. By then Erie   County officials also cited a failure of the state for nearly half a century to overhaul the state's social services laws to provide more efficient efforts against child abuse.

Violence young Western New York children in the early years of the 21st century prompted the state government's Office of Child and Family Services to begin intensely review the situation.

The later-day angels:

Aldifatah "Abdi" Mohamud, Gage Seneca, Erin Clayton Brooks, Austin Smith, Mayouna Smith, Jacob

T. Noe and Jay J. Bolvin in Niagara County, just north of Erie County, New York.

"ABDI": "Abdi" was 10, when he was fatally beaten on April 17, 2012 by his stepfather, Ali-Mohamed Mohamud.

The investigation of that boy's death shows that Mohamud, then working as a security officer for a private concern that dealt with many Buffalo area businesses, fatally "disciplined" the boy by striking him more than 70 times with a baker's hardwood rolling pin in the basement of their home on the East Side of Buffalo.

At the time of the fatal incident the 4 foot, 11-inch "Abdi" who weighed just under 100 pounds was a fifth- grader at Buffalo's International Preparatory School earning As and Bs.

During the fatal beating, a trial jury learned, his stepfather had stuffed a sock in his mouth which he then duct-taped closed. The jury also learned "Abdi's" his hands were bound with electrical code. The autopsy on the boy disclosed that the repeated blows from a baker's hardwood rolling pin had separated the boy's head from his spinal cord, the back his head was crushed and his brain was exposed outside his skull.

The trial jury also learned that "Abdi" had called 911 twice in the year before his death seeking protection from his disciplinarian stepfather, to no avail.

On the day of his murder "Abdi" had tried unsuccessfully to run away from his Guilford Street home after arguing with Mohamud about homework, an investigation of the family's situation disclosed.

"Abdi" couldn't get out of the house the day he was murdered.

By the time his mother came home the night from her night shift janitorial job at a big downtown Buffalo building she couldn't find him and called police to report him missing. But a police officer who came to the home after the woman's call ended up finding the dead boy in a pool of blood on the basement floor of the family home.

The State Supreme Court jury in the trial before Justice Christopher J. Burns learned from Dianne R. Vertes, then the Erie County government's chief medical examiner, that the extensive bruising she had found on the boy's body during his autopsy indicated he had been alive during much of the hours-long beating.

The jury learned the boy had been beaten for about 3 and one-half hours and, according to the medical examiner, and died sometime about 9 p.m.

The jury also told the sock Mohamud had taped over the boy's mouth had caused him to vomit from the blows to the head and there were ligature marks on one of his arms where he had been slashed by a knife.

During the trial the jury learned Mohamud, a native of Somalia, had met "Abdi" and the boy's Somali-born mother, Shukri Bile, two weeks after they had arrived in the U.S. from a Ugandan refugee camp in 2004.

On Oct. 18, 2012 the jury found the 41-year-old stepfather guilty of second-degree murder and on Nov. 15, 2012 the stepfather was sentenced to 25 years to life.

GAGE: Gage was the 3-year-old son of Justin Crouse's girlfriend who died at the hands of Crouse on the Cattaraugus Indian Reservation south of Buffalo on March 5, 2013.

Under a plea deal with the Erie County District Attorney's Office Crouse pleaded guilty in August 2013 to a reduced charge of first-degree manslaughter.

During the sentencing proceeding prosecutors noted county probation officers who had talked to Crouse before the sentencing found he seemed to have "limited remorse" what for he had done to the little boy.

And Crouse's own attorney, Emily P. Trott, conceded in court that "during the six to eight months that I represented Mr. Crouse, I have seen very little remorse for the action.

EAIN: Eain Clayton Brooks, 5, died on Sept. 17, 2013 after the latest instance in which he had been sodomized and beaten by his mother's boyfriend, Matthew W. Kuzdzal, 27 when they were in their West Side flat alone.

At that time the little boy's mother was pregnant with Kuzdzal's daughter. Nora Brooks gave birth to that girl on Oct. 3, 2013.

But the baby girl was placed in long-term foster care because Brooks had repeatedly told Erie County social workers, despite her own family's complaints, that Kuzdzal had no history of abusing Eain.

On Oct. 28, 2014 Kuzdzal, who had been sexually and physically abusing the little boy for about two years, was sentenced to 50 years to life.

Relatives of Eain's mother had been repeatedly complaining to Erie County child protection workers about Kuzdzal's frequent mistreating of the little boy.

Two caseworkers and two supervisors in that department were fired and top-level administrators in that unit were transferred after Eain's death.

AUSTIN: On Jan. 10, 2014 Dylan Schumacher, 17, was sentenced to 25 years to life for the March 19, 2013 fatal beating of Austin Smith, the 23-month-old son of his Springville, New York girlfriend as he was baby-sitting the boy and the boy's 3-month-old brother.

At the time of the murder Schumacher, who was not the father of either young child, was living in his own mother's house with his girlfriend and her to boys. A jury found Schumacher guilty for the extensive head injuries that took Austin's life.

MAYOUNA: Three-year-old Mayouna Smith died of blunt force trauma to her abdomen on Jan. 18, 2014 in the Allenhurst Drive flat in the Buffalo suburb of Amherst that she had shared with her mother, Ruhiyyih Shropshire, then 23, and her mother's then-boyfriend, Lamar Daniels, then 26, and the little girl's infant sister.

Amherst police were told by other apartment dwellers they could hear a little girl's screams from the Shropshire flat late on Jan. 17, 2014 and a man's voice, yelling and swearing for some reason.

Though the little girl's mother and boyfriend were the only two adults in the flat that night they insisted to police that they had no idea who fatally beat Mayouna.

An Erie County child protection services caseworker reported that the little girl's mother "appeared intimidated" by Daniels during the post- death investigation her agency conducted.

An autopsy showed the little girl had extensive bruising on her back, front, stomach, face, buttocks, arms, thighs, shoulders and genital area and old lacerations in her bowel and she had vaginal trauma from being sexually assaulted by someone.

Thanks to the efforts of The Buffalo News details of the troubled home life the little girl came out. The newspaper filed a Freedom of Information Request that disclosed the autopsy findings on the little girl.

The Buffalo News account of the autopsy, written by famed journalist Lou Michel, quoted the autopsy report as saying "The child was found to have extensive bruising on her back, front, stomach, face, buttocks, arms, thighs, shoulders and genital area and her death was the result of blunt force trauma to her internal organs." The autopsy report also noted "two lacerations to her bowel with both old and fresh injuries.

Additionally the child had vaginal trauma.

Though Mayouna's death was ruled a homicide as of the publication of this book no arrests had been made over her murder.

JAY: The horrors of child abuse so late into the 21st Century prompted New York State Governor Andrew M. Cuomo on July 29, 2013 to sign legislation creating Jay-J's Law which allowed for tougher penalties against offenders convicted of repeatedly abusing a child.

That development came as a result of the beatings a few years earlier of infant Jay J. Bolvin by his father, Jeremy Bolvin, 24, in the family's North Tonawanda home in Niagara County, just north of Erie County and the Buffalo, New York area.

Colvin went to prison but Jay J. suffered severe brain damage that left him with epilepsy and communication skill problems for literally the rest of his life.

The attacks on children in the Western part of New York State also lead the Erie County government to increase the availability of it child protection caseworkers to react to reports of child abuse or neglect from staff at Buffalo's two major hospital's dealing with child injuries, Women and Children's Hospital and Sisters Hospital.

Under Erie County Executive Mark C. Poloncarz in 2014 that Buffalo-based government's Department of Social Services hired more child protection case workers and upgraded training and oversight to deal with child abuse cases.

Based on an extensive review of the Erie County government's renewed emphasis on dealing with child abuse cases in 2014 the New York State government's Office of Children and Family Services, which had been critical of what it had found to be that government's "minimum amount of required work" dealing with such cases, cited the government's "more thorough" investigations of child safety episodes. But the state office's report chided by Erie County government for only having 80 child protection case workers on staff as it called on the government to "maintain the established higher standards" recently implemented on its handling of child abuse situations, including giving its caseworkers "sufficient time for completing the thorough investigations they are capable of."

CHAPTER TWENTY

But Problems Continued

JACOB: In an eerie replay of the Gail Trait horrors of 1978 on May 14, 2014 Jacob T. Noe, then 8, was stabbed to death by his mentally ill mother, Jessica L. Murphy, 30, two months after she had been under psychiatric care for her known bipolar disorder condition for a week at the Erie County Medical Center in Buffalo.

That had been her fourth hospitalization for her mental problems in about two years. And, it was learned later, that she had been taken to the Buffalo hospital for her latest treatment for her mental problems in March 2014 shortly after she had showed up at a Buffalo police station with Jacob and asked officers to protect the boy. That prompted her hospitalization and the boy's temporary placement with Murphy's estranged husband, with her getting the boy back after her brief March 2014 hospitalization

And Jacob's death came after a Erie County child protection caseworker had investigated the maritally- estranged woman's North Buffalo flat where she lived with her own mother and other relatives to ensure living conditions there were suitable.

Authorities reported that Jacob was pronounced death at Woman & Children's Hospital where he had been rushed soon after his mommy had repeatedly stabbed and choked him in her bedroom, severing his aortic artery.

Like Trait, Murphy told the first Buffalo police officers who rushed to the scene of that tragedy that she had killed her son to save him from going to hell.

On April 27, 2015 Murphy pleaded not responsible by reason of mental disease or defect. In October 2015 she was indefinitely committed to treatment at a state mental institution rather than standing trial on murder charges.

Jacob's dad filed a wrongful death suit over the government's handling of his estranged wife's mental problems and his son's plight when returned to the insane woman.

On May 23, 2014 then Erie County Executive Mark C. Poloncarz, the county government's top elected official, acknowledged the county's Child Protective Services unit continued to have serious operational problems. Disciplinary actions had been taken against its workers 33 time over the past year and five of its workers had been fired and nine others suspended for a time.

But Poloncarz denounced as a "scapegoat" attempt demands by two members of the Erie County Legislature, the county's law-making unit, that Carol Dankert-Maurer, then the county's commissioner of social services, be forced to resign. The resignation demands of Legislature Majority Leader Joseph C. Lorigo and Legislator Lynne M. Dixon came after it was revealed that a child protection worker had been scheduled to visit the north Buffalo home of Jacob Noe and his mother the day she killed the boy.

It came out that the investigation into Jacob's living conditions had tragically been put on hold because the caseworker who had previously been assigned to that case had been suspended without pay after failing to meet department standards in a large number of other cases earlier in the year.

Noting the number of problems the child protective services unit had been having Lorigo told the news media: "As many people have, I've grown frustrated learning about these deaths through the media. The Department of Social Services is $800 million of our $1.4 billion budget, and if Commissioner Dankert- Maurer is unable to do her job, which she has shown she is unable to do so, I think it's time for a change."

Poloncarz that same day told Buffalo News reporter Harold McNeil that "tragically" Jacob had been murdered by his mother "in the early morning hours of the day" a newly-assigned caseworker had been set to visit her home.

"The loss of any child's life is a tragedy, especially one taken in a violent manner, but our focus remains on preventing similar tragedies from occurring in the future," Poloncarz said.

Still, Lorigo complained that day that the social services commissioner had seemed to be spending more time in her then-role as president of the New York State Public Welfare Association then overseeing the operations in her department.

"It's my understanding that she spends the vast majority of her time dealing with that duty rather than her duties here in Erie County, which she is being paid for," Lorigo told McNeil. "If she is unable to spend the time to do the job of an $800 million county department, it's time of her to go," he added.

Poloncarz told McNeil and News reporter Lou Michel that same day that the social services department had been working diligently to improve its child protective responses but several recently hired caseworkers had either not passed their six-month probationary training or had been reprimanded, suspended or fired.

On June 19, 2014 the Erie County Legislature unanimously approved plans to hire 37 new workers to help the county's Child Protective Services unit cope with a still-growing backlog of cases involving complains of young children being maltreated

That action came amid reports that caseworkers had complained to county lawmakers of both the Democrat and Republican parties secretly about having to deal with heavy caseloads while working in a climate of fear and intimidation under the operation of the county's Social Service Department as it was then being run by Commissioner Carol Dankert-Maurer, an ally of County Executive Poloncarz.

News media reports at that time disclosed that one retired county child protection worker had told some county lawmakers that while Dankert-Maurer had publicly spoken about her concerns that child protection workers under her were burdened dealing with up to 40 or 50 active cases at a time the number of active cases being investigated by each caseworker then was closer to 100 for each worker, making it impossible to effectively deal with each report of abuse.

By June 2014 the Child Protective Services unit was dealing with 4,600 open cases, up from about 1,400 open cases in May 2013, a statistic that bothered county lawmakers of both major political parties.

That month the Erie County Legislature approved the Poloncarz' administration's request to hire 37 additional Child Protective Services workers to deal with the horrors.

Also that month the State Legislature passed child protection legislation requiring the state to track repeated reports of abuse and neglect of children received through the 24-hour telephone hotline the state government was then running to collect reports of the maltreatment of children.

The legislation was sponsored by State Senator Tim Kennedy, a Buffalo Democrat, who had been shocked to learn that the previous year a state audit of Erie County government child protective services investigation showed that 72 percent of those cases had involved complaints dealing with families with a history of previous child protective investigations in recent years, with nearly a quarter of those complaints involving families with five or more previous cases of alleged abuse of children in those homes.

In a civil lawsuit filed by the grandmother of 5-year- old Eain Clayton Brooks who was killed by the boyfriend of his mother Buffalo News reporter Lou Michel disclosed on Feb.

4, 2015 that Erie County government's child protective services workers had dismissed several reports from the boy's family and from professionals that he had been beaten, burned and abused for nearly two years before his death in September 2013.

Michel disclosed that on behalf of Robin Hart - the little boy's maternal grandmother - attorney Daniel J. Chiacchia found that complaints about the little boy's ultimately fatal situation came from staffers at the Gateway-Longview agency which ran an early- childhood education program where Eain had been sent to prepare him for elementary school work.

The Gateway-Longview staff, Chiacchia disclosed, had complained to the government unit four times about the little boy showing up for classes showing indications of having been injured while seated with a belt, showing signs of burns and scalding on his body, and coming once with a black eye, only to have each report of abuse inflicted on the boy dismissed by the county's child protective services staff.

With the horrors of abuse-caused deaths of Buffalo area children in the five years Dankert-Maurer had run the county's Social Services Department the county executive in January 2015 nominated her briefly to run the county's Department of Mental Health.

But amid complaints from the Republican majority of the County Legislature Poloncarz quickly withdrew her nomination, forcing her to remain head of the welfare agency until her successor, Dr. Al Dirschberger took over March 26, 2015.

Vice president, supervisor and administrator of child care services at the more than century-old Gateway- Longview non-profit agency of Western New York that provided special-education services to students with disabilities where he managed a $10 million annual budget, Dirschberger's county government job involved a five-year appointment.

Poloncarz took on the caseload problems by hiring the additional caseworkers, placing some in county schools and hospitals to better detect child abuse cases early on. He also hare 12 part-time former law enforcement workers to conduct investigations and to assist caseworkers in checking on child abuse situations.

Under the efforts of the County Legislature and the work of Poloncarz and Dirschberger by late 2015 the New York State Office of Children and Family Services congratulated the county government on its continuing efforts to deal with such problems.

In a written statement requested by The Buffalo News newspaper in October 2015 on the Erie County situation, that state office spoke of "...steady improvement in the way Erie County managed its CPS caseload and investigates reports of suspected child abuse and maltreatment."

The state agency also stressed that it was continuing to "work closely with the county to better train CPS workers, monitor and review open cases, and provide detailed feedback."

ACKNOWLEDGEMENTS

Daniel DiLandro, Buffalo State College archivist and special collections librarian; E.H. Butler Library, Buffalo State College, Buffalo, NY.; Buffalo Courier-Express newspaper, Buffalo, NY.; Buffalo Evening News, later Buffalo News, newspaper, Buffalo, NY.; Buffalo and Erie County, NY, Public Library; Newspaper Archive.com, the world's largest collection of newspaper archives online.

ABOUT THE AUTHOR

Matt Gryta, a Western New York journalist for over four decades, began his career with two years as editor-in-chief of the Buffalo State College RECORD. For over 40 years he served as a Buffalo News staff reporter. From 1970 through May 197, as a draftee who came into the U.S. Army with professional experience as a police reporter and general assignment reporter for what was then the Buffalo Evening News, he became a U.S. Army war correspondent in Vietnam as a sergeant heading the writers and photographers in the Public Information Office of the Americal Division. That division was the reactivated 23rd Infantry Division formed in May 1942 on the island of New Caledonia after the Japanese attack on Pearl Harbor. Its name was a contraction of "American, New Caledonian Division."

Gryta was one of the principal reporters covering the developments in the Trait case.

Among Gryta's other non-fiction books are:

The Real Teflon Don, the first public disclosure of the secret New York State Police unit that in the late 1960s until early in the next decade successfully tape- recorded the telephone conversations of upper limits of the crime empire of Mafia co- founder Stefano Magaddino and his chief operatives.

Joey 22, the full story of Joe Christopher, the Buffalo-raised racial serial killer of Black and Latino men late in the 20th Century.

A Death In Buffalo, which covers the death of Richard Yancey Long Jr. at the hands of two off-duty Buffalo, New York, police officers and their tobacco-salesman friend.